A BOUQUET OF BUSINESS CASE STUDIES

ASM Group of Institutes
Pune India

First published in 2020 by

Becomeshakespeare.com

One Point Six Technologies Pvt Ltd.
119-123, 1st Floor, Building J2, B - Wing, WadalaTruck Terminal,
Wadala East, Mumbai, Maharashtra, India, 400022.
T:+91 8080226699

ISBN - 978-93-90543-35-9

FOREWORD

I am pleased to write this foreword to the first ever Case Study Volume published by Audyogik Shikshan Manadal's (ASM Group of Institutes) which as I know is one of highly progressive group offering educational opportunities to all potential students from KG to PG levels.

The major emphasis and uniqueness of this publication of Case Volumes vindicates ASM's claim of being one of the pioneers in the adoption of Case methodology as an essential feature of its pedagogy and the proficiency of the faculty in developing interesting case studies in all aspects of business management more so on Indian business scenario

Another important contribution of these Case Volumes is the Live Case Studies on ongoing business units in India and the immense variety of Case Studies on current business scenario from all segments and functions in India's vast Industry base. The Case Volumes look like a Colorful 'bouquet' of Case Studies offering rich combination of subject and topic oriented Cases developed based on secondary data

I am sure that the ASM Case Volumes will be rich resource for the academicians, students and the practicing executives and will prove to be yet another mile stone achievement by the progressive team of management at ASM Group of Institutes

Dr. Bhimaraya Metri

Director

Indian Institute of Management Nagpur

CONTENTS

PREFACE

ASM Group Publication of Case Volumes

Business Case Studies and Their Relevance to Management Education

Many B-schools outside India have adopted decades ago the case study methodology for teaching almost all branches of management studies. This trend has been seen in India also, wherein a majority of the Indian Institutes of Management (IIMs) have implemented case study–based methodology as an important pedagogical tool in business management education. The major issue in India is, however, the inadequate interaction between B-schools and industries. The fault lies with both B-schools and the industry. The B-schools in a majority of cases cannot provide research-based solutions to industry problems due to a lack of necessary infrastructure and facilities. And the industries in the absence of any direct benefit from the institutes are not inclined to waste their time and funds on B-school education.

Hence, there is a severe shortage in Indian case studies through which the B-schools can provide industry insight to its students. Majority of these case studies are from situations in industries in foreign countries and have very little relevance to Indian students who need to study the situations in the Indian industries

Besides, the objectives and purposes for which case studies are developed abroad are much different from the level and course of studies in Indian B-schools. Therefore, the dependence on foreign case studies for Indian students does not provide any real situational insight on Indian business. Although the syllabus for management studies requires taking the students through casestudy methodology, unfortunately there are not many Indian case studies that can be discussed with the students.

Thus, it is a Catch-22 situation. Unless institutes have the capability and the required infrastructure to cater to industry-related issues, they cannot expect any interactive support from the industries; unless institutes get adequate data from industries, their teaching content and quality continue to be much less than the expectations of the industry from students who pass out from such institutes.

Objectives of use of case study methodology

The main objectives of using case-based teaching as a major pedagogical tool in B-schools are as follows:

1. To facilitate students' concept development capabilities through exposure to real-life problems in Industries

2. To enable students to correlate theoretical topics with the techniques used in analysing complex issues in business situations

3. To develop skills using which students can develop application matrix for the theoretical topics for real-life problem analysis and resolution techniques

4. Help the students of B-schools to develop orientation towards the important attributes and attitudinal requirements for effective handling of complex situations at the workplace

5. To develop a clear understanding of the techniques used for problem analysis, situation analysis and decision analysis and appropriate understanding of the difference between problems and situations in management

6. To develop the group-based approaches to solving problems and challenges at the workplace by appropriate coordination of and collaboration with all related aspects of a situation

7. To develop a reference manual for recording the problems tackled and the essential lessons learnt from past incidences for use in future eventualities of recurrence of issues

8. To develop the preventive steps that must be initiated to ensure the problems resolved once do not recur in the immediate future

Types of case studies

The entire gamut of business case studies can be classified as follows:

1. Evaluative case studies-Teaching Case

2. Task- or action-oriented case studies (including project-based case studies)

3. Research-oriented case studies -Case Research

Teaching case studies are basically oriented towards developing the evaluative and analytical skills of students towards industry situations. Such case studies draw the attention of participants of the case resolution methodology on the in-depth correlative evaluation of the issues in the case study with the various related topics that the students have to study about in their classrooms. These case studies could be on issues related to human resources, industrial relations, product and process, marketing and finance management areas in business management.

Such case studies help the students mainly to examine their understanding of evaluative steps such as evaluation of the financial situation of a company or the quality aspects of its products and services, etc. The task- or action-oriented case studies dwell on business issues that call for appropriate decision-making capabilities of executives. By involving students of management studies in the resolution activity of such case studies, the skills learnt by them through the theoretical studies can be experimented in the resolution exercises.

The students can be motivated to apply their decision-making skills along with their risk management ability to make business decisions. Developing a plan of actions oriented towards the resolution of the case issues calls for effective role-play techniques as also presentation skills from the part of students; they are normally required to defend their plan of approach and decisions in front of other students and the faculty, which helps them improve their capabilities to sustain questions and criticisms, normal features in business management.

Research-based case studies, as the name suggests, involve students in research initiatives to establish a hypothesis or to disprove a common belief, which influence the progress and sustenance of business ideologies or even scientific or technical aspects of business dynamics. These case studies normally call for pre requisites such as thorough business knowledge and enough exposure to both the theoretical and practical aspects of the issues presented in the case studies. Issues of corporate governance and social welfare functions, which have both obligatory and voluntary elements attached to them, are pursued in research studies to establish the utility purposes of such aspects, which range from free will to a compelled activity.

However, the real problem today for B-schools is the non-availability of good case studies on Indian business. The age of imported case studies is fast losing its relevance to the Indian business scenario, which in itself has unique features among the global economies the usage of imported case studies from foreign businesses is fast losing its relevance to the Indian business scenario, which in itself has unique features among the global economies. India, which is rated as the world's fourth largest economy, definitely needs specific and separate approaches to the case study methodology as a pedagogical tool for B-school studies.

Present Environment

The Academic Environment across the world to is facing a major disruption on account the global pandemic COVID 19 forcing the Off line education to switch over to Online/Blended versions of Teaching and learning process. And use of Case methodology and simulation exercises are the main ingradients while maintaining the effective ways of delivering experiential learning through use of Case and case lets in an online mode of teaching ensuring student engagements and online interactive ways of knowledge dissemination. Realising this requirement even globally reputed Institutes such as Harvard & MIT Sloan have made Case method of teaching as essential parts of their online courses

ASM Group with nearly 250 business Case Studies developed by its faculty over years takes pleasure in offering these Cases mostly on Indian businesses through these Case volumes to the faculty, students as also for Executive Education programs. The Case Studies are selected from ASM's Captive Case Bank as most appropriate for the current day syllabi and on Indian Business Scenario including select Live Case Studies on ongoing businesses

ASM group is certain that the Case Volumes as published will receive excellent response from the faculty and students alike in B schools in India and abroad.

From The Author's Desk

ASM Group of Institutes is pleased and proud to offer their second Text / Reference Book on Business Case Studies in the form of case Volumes with diligently chosen and edited set of Business Case Studies in the form of a beautiful bouquet consisting of case studies on all specialization areas like HR, Marketing Finance and Operations Management. Few Live Case Studies on ongoing industries from india and abroad provide additional value like icing on the cake.

All the Case Studies are developed in house by ASM faculty based on secondary data from public domain and primary data through discussions.

Dr. Sandeep Pachpande

An academician, entrepreneur real estate developer techno preneur, mentor, author, keynote speaker, agriculturist, and visionary Dr. Sandeep Pachpande brings a multi-faceted business sense to the table every day. With a vision to provide global standards of education combined with the strength of industry exposure, binds his avid leadership that has guided and mentored the career of thousands of students.

A Computer Engineer Dr. Sandeep Pachpande is Harvard Business School alumni & done executive programs from Kellogg, Babson, and is Gold Medalist in MBA from Leeds Metropolitan University, UK. He is a Ph.D. guide, keynote speaker has authored many books, and has traveled to 36 countries on various assignments, conferences, seminars, study tours, and delegations, and is truly global in his thought, words & deeds.

Prof. J. A. Kulkarni

Prof. J. A. Kulkarni brings along with him nearly 40 years of industry experience at senior levels including Tata Motors, M&M Ltd., and Bajaj Auto ltd. He is a University Gold Medalist for his BE in Mech Engineering and backed up by a post-graduate education in management from Germany.

Prof. Kulkarni during his 16 years of experience with ASM Group of Institutes specializes in teaching the MBA students in subjects such as Strategic Management and Sustainability.

Prof. Kulkarni's major contribution has been in the development of an unique case resolution method and in the development of several business Case Studies.

Prof. Kulkarni has authored book on Business Case Studies as also on Innovative Management and contributed more than 25 Research Papers for National and International Conferences. Prof. Kulkarni has visited several countries on business negotiations and also as visiting faculty on a few of the foreign universities. Prof. J. A. Kulkarni is nominated as Board of ISODC USA as International Director and has participated in several international conferences and organizing workshops/ conferences and case competitions

The Co-Authors

All the authors are faculty from ASM Group of Institutes with rich experience in the use of case methodology of teaching and have decades of teaching experience at ASM Group of Institutes.

Dr. Sanjay Dharmadhikari

Dr. Sanjay Dharmadhikari has 22 years of rich Industry experience along with meritorious 12 years in academics as Director in several prestigious Institutes is currently engaged as Professor and Dean Academics at ASM Group of Institutes, Pune.

Dr. Dharmadhikari has contributed several research papers for national and international conferences and also authored a few books in Management.

Dr. Dharmadhikari during his academic tenure has held major responsibilities assigned at the university level for the implementation of pedagogical systems and procedures.

Dr. Sandip Sane

Dr. Sandip Sane has a Masters in Management with nearly 15 years of experience at Director levels in Institutes of repute. Dr. Sane has contributed several Research papers for National International conferences.

Dr. Sandip Sane is currently the Director for the state of art PGDM course of studies at ASM IBMR, Pune. Dr. Sandip Sane specializes in Business Strategy as a subject of studies as also a Mentor for the post graduate student in Management Studies.

Dr. Satish Pawar

Dr. Satish Pawar is presently the Professor and Director of Research at ASM Group of Institutes research cell. Dr. Satish is an approved guide for Ph.D. Scholars of SPPU

Dr.Satish Pawar has nearly 20 years of rich experience as a professor for the MBA.

MCA, MD MBBS, and BSc Courses of studies at distinguished Institutes in India.

Dr. Satish Pawar has contributed 30 research papers in National and International Journals and Conferences and has authored 4 in Management and Research

CASE STUDIES

Case Study no1

1. Corporate Governance – It's Implications

A case study on The 'Infrastructure Leasing & Financial Services' Episode

Learning Objectives

Corporate governance and its implications are not just restricted to board room discussions especially in case of financial institutions. Reason for this is they implicate the financial markets due to which they have larger public repercussions. This creates external implications as money invested in financial markets is done by general public and not by the financial institution. So governance plays an important role within and outside the firms.

Synopsis

Financial woes of the Indian economy continue in spite of taking strong measures. In 2009 Satyam fiasco rocked the stock markets and similar type of incident has taken place in 2018. Stock markets were flying high and bullish trend was present in markets in September 2018 up to 3 rd week. Then the markets showed a downward trend and speculations were made regarding the reasons for the same.

With the future stability of the Indian financial system on the line, executives running a giant infrastructure lender gathered at the company's glassy, modernist headquarters in Mumbai and hammered out an ambitious restructuring plan in September last week to manage a $12.6 billion debt burden after a string of defaults.

Except that they weren't really calling the shots any more. The very next day, the government in New Delhi authorized a move to sweep in and seize control of Infrastructure Leasing & Financial Services Ltd., a vast conglomerate that's raised billions of dollars in the corporate bond market and powered the nation's public project building boom.

The stunning move, more typical of China's command-and-control economy than a free-wheeling democracy like India, caught investors by surprise

The decision to oust the company's board was taken after the government had quietly reached out, at least two days earlier, to former bureaucrats and current bankers to orchestrate a board coup, according to people familiar with the matter. The government had been monitoring the lender for two weeks, one of the people said.

Following a series of meetings in September and months after the first defaults by the systemically important lender, the ministry was worried about the multiple shocks to the financial markets that would follow from IL&FS's collapse.

"The restoration of confidence of the money, debt and capital markets, the banks and financial institutions in the credibility and financial solvency of the IL&FS Group is of utmost importance for the financial stability of capital and financial markets," the government said in a statement

The case details

What is IL&FS?

Infrastructure Leasing & Financial Services ltd one of the oldest infrastructure services had in the past helped out many projects in India. To their credit to name a few Chenani-Nashri Tunnel (or Patnitop Tunnel) in Udhampur Built at the foot of the Himalayan Mountains, the 9km-long Patnitop tunnel connects the districts of Chenani and Nashri. The project involved an investment of Rs37.2bn ($723m). Also many road projects have been built by them. The investors in this include LIC & SBI. It has a long list of subsidiaries.

The case is of peculiar nature of IL&FS. It is supposed to be a private company, which acts like a quasi-government arm because it lends to the infrastructure sector and has a lot of big government companies and banks as shareholders More importantly, it is both a lending institution as well as an execution company. It has bid, won and taken on projects under various subsidiaries, and which in turn have raised debt financing both from the parent as well as from the market. The subsidiaries were needed to be created because the government regulations mandate that each concession based infrastructure project needs a separate entity because loans are taken specific to that entity and project. With IL&FS taking on so many projects, it became a highly opaque structure with the government as a partner in most of its projects, which gave many the feeling of comfort that the risks were underwritten by the government. And it had a management team, which successfully hid the rising crisis and tried to bury it under the carpet until it could no longer do so.

A loan of a ₹1,000-crore from the Small Industries Development Bank of India (SIDBI) on 13 September had been defaulted. The person who was heading the firm Mr. Ravi Parthasarathy quit the company giving health reasons. On 17 September, rating agency ICRA downgraded IL&FS's credit rating to default after it failed to meet repayment obligations of ₹12,000 crore in short-term and long-term borrowings.

With cash crunch and falling stock markets the company started missing on payments. Commercial papers payments were missed and suddenly the markets and lenders started getting the indication that all is not well. Banks, mutual and pension fund managers, insurers and individuals are bracing for further losses. Among the concerns for investors is that IL&FS has made loans to its own units. The company is also in default on short-term borrowings known as inter-corporate deposits.

Then the news of DSP Mutual Fund selling DHFL's one-year ₹300-crore paper at 11% and the subsequent fear of a contagion effect spooked the market. DSP Investment Managers Pvt Ltd later clarified it had no credit issue with DHFL and was just trying to reduce its portfolio maturity. The DHFL management also said that it had not defaulted on any bonds or repayment, nor had there been any instance of delay on repayment of any liability. The management of DHFL said it did not have any exposure to IL&FS.

RBI smelt something fishy and an audit was initiated. The report cited many lapses and in mean time the bonds on which payments were due did not take place. This created panic and the secrets came out in to the open. At this point the share market also saw a downfall with cash crunch and prices started falling down.

The shareholding and the projects and the dozens of subsidiaries that made things even more complicated for rating agencies as well as auditors, though they should have been more vigilant given the problems that all infrastructure companies are facing. To be fair to the credit rating agencies, they had flagged off a warning, though inexplicably, perhaps lulled by the blue chip projects, its partners, and its quasi-government nature; they failed to downgrade the debt early enough until the defaults actually started.

OUTCOME:

On October 1st2018 the government announced that it is taking control of the management of IL&FS, whose loans and debentures have been downgraded to default status by rating agency ICRA. The Mumbai National Company Law Tribunal– a quasi-judicial body that decides on issues relating to Indian companies – allowed India's ministry of corporate affairs to replace the company's board with a new one.

The existing management of IL&FS has been replaced with a new six-member board, which will be helmed by Mr.Uday Kotak, managing director of Kotak Mahindra Bank.

Other members include Mr.Vineet Nayyar, executive vice chairman of the IT services company Tech Mahindra; Mr.GN Bajpai, former chief of India's market regulator Securities and Exchange Board of India, former ICICI Bank chairman Mr.GC Chaturvedi, and former IAS officers Mr.Malini Shankar and Mr.Nanda Kishore.

But unlike Lehman, the government has already indicated that IL&FS is not going to be allowed to collapse. The rescue plan is already in place and its shareholders like LIC and SBI are ready to give it enough money to meet its repayment obligations.

However, the IL&FS case should be a wakeup call for the government precisely for the reason that it reached a stage of collapse without anyone spotting the problem early on. Unlike the case of banks, where the Reserve Bank of India (RBI) had spotted the problems early on, and where it had prodded them to recognize the bad debts and clean up balance sheets, the IL&FS case shows the gaps that exist in our financial systems especially asset liability mismatches or the credit risk in the NBFC space even now, which need to be plugged quickly.

FUTURE

What are the lessons going forward? One is of course that it makes little sense to have an NBFC, which also is in the business of actually executing infrastructure projects. A pure lending agency would have probably been monitored more closely by the RBI. Equally, execution agencies about to get into cash flow trouble are far easier to spot because they are also not raising debt as a lending NBFC.

Another point is that the government does need to figure out why so many infrastructure projects run into cash flow and other financial problems (which in turn creates problems for their lenders). This is a bigger problem because infrastructure is a long gestation business, while finances raised are for shorter tenures thus causing asset liability and cash flow mismatches.

Finally, it might make best sense to slowly wind up the IL&FS business after selling off its debt and paying of its asset instead of letting it exist with a rap on the knuckles.

The tide seems to have turned in favour of commercial banks: the liquidity crunch following the IL&FS crisis has pushed corporate borrowers away from the bond markets, back to banks.

Data released by the Reserve Bank of India (RBI) on 24 October shows non-food credit growth at over a four-year high of 14.5% year-on-year (y-o-y) for the fortnight ended 12 October. In absolute terms, non-food credit grew from ₹78.15 trillion in the fortnight ended 13 October 2017 to ₹89.47 trillion in the 12 October 2018 fortnight.

Bankers are upbeat about the growth in credit and said corporate borrowers are returning as bond markets turn risk averse.

"The gap between bank lending rates and the borrowing rates from the bond market has considerably narrowed now. Moreover, in some cases, bank loans are turning out to be cheaper than bonds," said P.K. Gupta, managing director, State Bank of India (SBI).

The current credit apprehension in the bond markets has been beneficial to banks as borrowers have started preferring bank loans over bonds, according to Mr.AjayManglunia, head (fixed income advisory), Edelweiss Financial Services.

"Banks have cashed in on the opportunity presented by the falling risk appetite of the bond market after the IL&FS crisis.

Investors are going slow on investing in financial companies and that has led to higher spreads for other bond issuers as well at this moment," said Mr.Manglunia. He said that AA-rated borrower can raise funds from the bond market at 9.5-10% now, up from 8.5% a year ago.

Conclusions

The IL&FS crisis has thrown the business of Non-Banking Financial Companies (NBFCs) in disarray. With liquidity becoming an issue, the parallels between an approaching winter and the chill that is setting in on small business financing is being talked about in great detail.

Lenders are not sure if there are any more skeletons in the closet and every payment and repayment schedule of an NBFC is being scrutinized threadbare for any signs of distress. Mutual funds, which made a killing in the last three years, have also decided to go slow on exposure to NBFCs. As a result, there is suddenly a severe liquidity crisis in the sector and this is bound to have an impact on small business in the country. SMEs in the country have become reliant on NBFCs to fund their needs and there is a fear that with liquidity being an issue, these small businesses would find it very tough to raise money. As a result, thousands of jobs would now be at risk. The task for the new board, then, is cut out – to raise long-term equity to pull the company out ofthe woods.

Case Questions

1. Government has reacted to the situation but can it solve the problem. The shadow bank is a financial behemoth with

assets in excess of Rs 1.15 lakh crore ($16 billion) and debt of Rs 91,000 crore.

2. What should be the precautions to be taken in future from audit view to ensure such repercussions do not take place?

2. Marriage of Convenience

A Case Study on Jet-Etihad deal

Learning Objectives:

Mergers and acquisitions have become one of the most well-known business strategies in the global economy. Increasing market share, gaining core capabilities, and accessing more capital at lower cost are results from a successful and effective merger and acquisition. However, emphasizing business strategies and financial issues is not enough. Organizations also need to focus on their human resources in mergers and acquisitions. Knowledge and knowledge management as a soft side of mergers and acquisitions play a vital role. Having a better understanding of the relationship between knowledge management and mergers and acquisitions will help the combined organization succeed in mergers and acquisitions and sustain competitive advantage.

Synopsis:

Airlines business has started to lose its charm as operative expenses have become very high. Added to this competition has increased and also customer's expectations have gone up. Jet airways have tried every possible manner of survivability and when it found the going difficult started looking for partners. In this situation another airline was looking for expansion and wanted to do so in time of crisis as the valuation would be suitable the airline is Etihad. This case deals how the marriage can be a win-win situation for both of them.

History:

Jet Airways Ltd. soared to unprecedented heights at the beginning of the current millennium. And then calamity struck in the form of the global financial meltdown of 2008 which brought many mighty corporations to their knees. Downturn in economic activity impacted Jet's performance, bringing it to the brink of failure. The management at Jet was left grappling with many operational and personnel related challenges. It was a time for Jet to take certain tough decisions. And it did make them. With the opening up of India's aviation sector for foreign direct investment, Jet became the first Indian flier to seek foreign alliance.

Etihad airlines were started by started by a Royal (Amiri) Decree by Sheikh Khalifa bin Zayed Al Nahyan as a flagship carrier for the United Arab Emirates in July 2003. In a short period in 2011they had reported a net profit of USD14 million. In 2013, Etihad reported third consecutive net profit USD   62 million up 48 per cent from the previous year. They were looking for expansion of operations.

Analysts were quick to conclude that Etihad was very close to picking up a stake in the Mr.Naresh Goyal-controlled Jet Airways. The possibility of a deal, naturally, pushed up Jet Airways share price. While no financial details of the deal have been forthcoming, experts say that the Abu Dhabi-based airlines will pick up a 24 per cent stake in Jet Airways for over $300 million.

After all, the market last year shrank 8-10 per cent due to high fares, and full-service carrier Kingfisher Airlines had to close its service as it was unable to face the onslaught of low-cost carriers which have grabbed over 65 per cent of the market. Even Jet Airways, a full-service carrier, in order to maintain its market share, was impelled to revamp its operations moving nearly 60 per cent of its domestic capacity and offer it at low fares under Jet Konnect. The only silver lining has been that airlines have temporarily cashed in on the vacuum left by Kingfisher Airlines' exit by increasing fares. But the question is how long can it last if passenger growth continues to falter?

Clearly, the sector is not out of the woods. So why is Etihad so keen to put in its money into Jet Airways, especially when the global aviation industry, too, is under a cloud? The answer is simple: Etihad wants to expand in a slowdown when valuations are low; once the market booms, it will be ready with expanded capacity. The airline has always been a pygmy compared to the big boys like Emirates and Qatar which rule the West Asian market. It has a fleet of 67 aircraft, which is nearly a third of Emirates and half of Qatar. In India, too, with less than 2 per cent of the international market, it is a minor player compared to Emirates (over 13 per cent share) and Qatar (over 5 per cent). Etihad has 52 weekly flights to and from India, which is way below Emirates (185 flights) and Qatar (95 flights).

This is why Etihad has always followed a different track from the big boys – to survive and expand. The first key element of its three- pronged strategy is to go in for a bevy of code share agreements. Thus, Etihad has signed up such agreements with over 41 airlines across the globe (compared to only ten by Emirates), which has helped it get additional passengers on its network. Two, it has taken its relationship with these partner airlines to the next level by jointly marketing routes with them. And three, it has taken equity stakes in some of its key airline partners. It has already done so with four: 10 per cent in Virgin Australia, 29 per cent in air Berlin, less than 3 per cent in Dublin-based Aer Lingus and, the latest, 40 per cent in Air Seychelles. These alliances have, of course, paid good dividends. For instance, air Berlin generated over 300,000 additional passengers on the network of the two airlines and also revenues of over 100 million pounds.

It is a similar gain that Etihad and Jet hope will happen when they eventually tie the knot. Etihad's chief executive, James

Hogan, has made no bones that Asia, particularly India and China, would be the key markets in the days to come. And he has already hinted that he will be looking at "one or two strategic investments" which could be in Asia. He also has in-house talent to help in understanding Jet Airways, as his new CEO of air Berlin is none other than WolfangProck-Schauer who was earlier hired by Goyal to run Jet Airways.

The Case details

Jet Airways already has an ongoing relationship with Etihad: a code share agreement in India for seven cities and also on the Paris route. This relationship would now be strengthened as part of the airline's overall global strategy. Etihad can feed in passengers seamlessly from Abu Dhabi across the country by using Jet Airways' wide coverage of over 53 cities in India. Currently, Etihad operates to only ten cities in India. Similarly, Jet could bring in passengers from Indian cities to Abu Dhabi, from where they could travel to any destination in West Asia and Africa where Etihad has excellent connectivity.

Jet Airways can also leverage Etihad's strong presence in Europe by bringing in Indian passengers through Abu Dhabi. That is a win-win for both sides as Jet currently operates only to Brussels, Milan and London in Europe on its own. (Through code-share agreements with Brussels Airlines and Thalys, it offers seamless connectivity to another 14 cities.) Etihad, on the other hand, has a huge network in Europe; it directly flies to over 17 destinations and through its elaborate code-share agreements with around 13 airlines offers seamless connectivity to over 88 cities. That, of course, is not the only route which could be an advantage to both the airlines. The India-North America market is one of the largest and most lucrative in terms of business. Jet Airways currently flies only to Newark and Toronto and through its code-share with United and Air Canada offers connectivity to all key markets in North America. But Etihad can provide an alternative to Indian flyers – they can fly seamlessly from Abu Dhabi to Chicago, New York and Washington, apart fromToronto. And through its code share agreement with American Airlines, it would allow Indians to fly all over the US.

Effects:

The agreement could also save costs. The two airlines could leverage their clout while buying fuel; they could also leverage their bargaining power with Boeing as Etihad has just ordered 50 aircraft from the American company, the bulk of which include the Dream liners, in association with Air Berlin. Jet Airways, of course, also has a fleet that comprises mostly of Boeings aircraft and could therefore work out similar integrated deals in the future. Also, the two could pare costs by using each other's ground operations at their hubs. Of course, Etihad would also need to resolve a key problem which it will soon face: to expand its operations in India, it will require more bilateral as currently as much as 85 per cent of the seats have been exhausted. Also the tie up analyst say could eat into Air India's business in the Middle East as well as in the US and Europe. Analysts say that the Indian government has been chary in opening up the bilateral with Dubai as well as other West Asian states in order to protect Air India. However, a friendly Indian partner could always be of help in convincing the government, say analysts.

Conclusions:

The scenario as it stands shows that it is clearly a marriage where everyone will be a winner of shares in Jet by Etihad shall be helpful for Jet as the cash striving airlines can hope to survive and get new lease of life. It depends on clearance from the authorities and how much faith is shown by both parties on each other. For survival of jobs of many employees and confidence in business to stay it is necessary for the deal to take place and clearly a marriage where everyone will be a winner to happen.

Case Questions:

1. What are the circumstances that lead to the fall of the airlines which was doing extremely well?

2. Can a merger or acquisition be enough to turn around business or other factors are also important.

3. In a larger picture is survivability of air line industry in the country at stake.

3. Scope for Growth Strategies in Emerging Markets

A case study of Nokia and Infosys

Learning Objectives:

1. To understand marketing strategies of Nokia and Infosys.

2. To study demand dynamics of the rural mobile handset market in India.

3. To analyse growth strategies adopted by the global players.

4. To understand SWOT analysis of Nokia and Infosys.

5. To help decision making through formulate growth strategy in emerging market.

Synopsis:

Should one focus on technology upgrading, emerging markets or both- a case of *mobile handset* major *Nokia* and the home-grown IT services major *Infosys*. At the start of 2010, Nokia commanded a 39% market share of the smart phone segment globally, which plummeted to below 5% in 2013. Its global market share in the overall mobile handset market slipped from 36.4% in 2009 to 28.9% in 2010, and eventually, a mere 14% in 2013. According to the Fortune list 2006 survey, Nokia was the 20th most admirable company in the world. Infosys was founded in 1981. The first Indian company to be listed on NASDAC, Infosys, chose high margins over fast growth, a strategy that has cost it both market capitalization and market share. In 2020 if we look at the growth strategy what do these two companies stand for? Moreover, should growth strategy be to focus on the developed markets, emerging markets, or both?

1. Industry Facts:

In 2006, Nokia, the world's largest producer of mobile phones, was the market leader in India with 78.8% of the market share. Since its entry into Indian mobile market in 1995, it focused on manufacturing of mobile handsets based on GSM technology. Nokia built a strong brand image with focused marketing and distribution network. It started focusing on the low-cost mobile phone segment for rural markets in India, but, faced stiff competition from Sony Ericsson, Samsung, and Motorola who also started offering low-cost handsets. Nokia's underdeveloped infrastructural facilities and low coverage were the biggest challenges for it to reach rural customers. The case facilitates a discussion on whether Nokia will be able to improve its performance and sustain its leadership position in India.

Infosys expects to grow at a faster pace in the current financial year than in 2017-18. The company, after posting a 2.2% sequential increase in dollar revenue during the October- December period, raised its revenue outlook for 2018-19 to 8.5- 9% in constant currency terms. Infosys's revenue grew 5.8% in constant currency terms in financial year 2017-18. It has to be a consultative-led selling approach," said Mark Livingston, Infosys's head of consulting. Infosys, like its peers, gets the bulk of its business from its largest clients: the top 25 clients accounted for a third or $1 billion of Infosys's $2.98 billion in revenue in the October-December quarter. In the quarter ended December 2017, just before Parekh took over as CEO, the top 25 customers accounted for 35.3% or $972.5 million of Infosys's$2.75 billion in revenue.

2. Emerging Market Trend:

Nokia today outlined its vision and strategic priorities for ensuring sustainable growth in its core businesses and tapping new opportunities in fast-growing markets. Nokia has employed the cost leadership strategy such as Purchasing power low in emerging markets hence Nokia provided cost effective products successfully, only 20% of the emerging market were not first time purchasers and People of emerging markets wanted value added services bundled with the phone. "Nokia is extremely well-positioned to win in its primary market with communication service providers, and we aim to target superior returns through focused growth into more attractive adjacent markets where high-performance, end-to-end networks are increasingly in demand.

Geographically, Infosys is aiming to split its revenues so that the US accounts for 40%; Europe, 40% and the rest of the world, 20%. Currently the American market accounts for a meaty 65%, Europe a fast growing 21% and the rest of the world, 14%. Infosys is repositioning itself with more focus on intellectual property and solution development, as well as on reusing technologies. "The old model was very lenient, you add more people, you get more revenue, you add more people, you get more revenue. You can't do that ad infinitum, it's not the way to build a sustainable business which will last for hundreds of years

3. SWOT Assessment:

Nokia is very strong brand name and positive image Strong distribution network Best Navigation (Nokia OVI Maps) Phones were not always good as competitors E.g.- in 2003, company was too late with clamshell models. Introductory phones were not user friendly, couldn't attain expected success Companies like Samsung, Sony and Motorola were eating into Nokia's market share New Operating Systems were putting Nokia into back foot Have high competitive advantage in terms of brand recognition and large market penetration With little innovation and existing low prices, company can improve market position S W T O

Infosys: Majority clients are based out of North America and Europe. It provides strong end to end business solutions. Infosys has strategic associated partner with major technology and business players to strengthen its services and business solutions. The company has earlier partnered with HP, IBM, Microsoft and Amazon etc. The strong partnership network allows Infosys to deliver innovative and collaborative solutions. Weaknesses are limited markets, lack of services for most of the emerging nations and thus missing out on a potential of growth. Infosys is one of the tech companies in India which has been a victim of the high attrition rate. Many employees leave for better career opportunities and higher education. High attrition rates affect company's image. Infosys has been identifying potential and investing heavily in early stage technology companies. Infosys has increased its focus on providing digital transformation services and thus increased global spending can be beneficial for it. Focusing on emerging markets, which are expected to give good business to IT services and consultancy firms in the future, Infosys should not fall behind when the opportunity is up for grabs. The IT services industry is a highly competitive industry. Infosys competes with large technology and consultancy firms like Accenture, Capgemini and TCS. For companies like Infosys, lower wage cost is a great competitive advantage, but there is a pressure of rising wages in India as well.

Outcomes:

The new generation of managers would be able to think in a rational way and change their mind-set supported by a bureaucratic organisational form. Leaning on a superior technological competence within the mobile phone sector, will be capable of ultimately becoming the market leader. Focus should be given to software and applications both. The present case will help to the businessman to describe solutions and choose best alternatives for the problems. Using SWOT analysis student should be focusing on the analytical approach to understand complexities and would help to improve strategic learning skills.

Conclusions:

After finishing mobile telecom network market Nokia has joined hands with IT services firm Infosys to develop solutions powered by new-age technologies like artificial intelligence (AI) and Machine Learning (ML) and "Infosys has built platforms that have become the new channels of growth for this extremely fast paced high growth logistics organization improving valuation and profitability.

Case Questions

Analyse the fact and answer the following questions.

1. Suggest an appropriate name for this case study?

2. Differentiate and distinguish growth strategies in the current scenario?

3. Develop a suitable blend for business growth?

4. The Price of Owning a CAT

A Case study in International acquisition-Growth Strategy'

Learning Objectives:

1. To understand how valuation of brand is done in international market.

2. To know more about the international environmental factors affecting profitability of the firm.

3. To understand the concept of economics of scale and its impact on financial health of an organization.

4. To know more about Merger and acquisition strategy of business expansion in international market.

5. To understand financial implications of Merger and Acquisition.

6. To know, what is the right time to acquire an international firm?

7. To understand the importance of synergies among merging organization for success of the merger.

Synopsis:

This case study discusses the acquisition of herculean automobile giant JLR by an Indian Automobile company TATA motors. Prior acquisition by Ford motors; Jaguar and Land Rover were owned by British multinational automobile company, 'British Leyland'. Ford first acquired Jaguar brand in 1983 for \$2.5 billion and then Land Rover 2000 for \$2.7 billion brand from of the list. Besides all this Jaguar & Land Rover vehicles had failed to impress buyers in the US & the Asian markets.

The TATA's Status: The Tata's were in the commercial vehicle segment for nearly 60 years and the passenger cars segment has been a very recent territory they have entered in late 90's. In view of the new product for an altogether new customer profile, Tata's have faced major performance equality problems in the small car segment, and only towards 2005 they have been able to lick all these niggling problems, and have introduced the Sedan version of the Indica also simultaneously upgrading the base model Indica to the V2 & the VISTA model which have established a fare amount of confidence in its customers, however they still lack their competition in terms of customer satisfaction levels & the niggling product quality issues. There exists a limitation up to which the Tata's can stretch their capability in the indigenous design & development of cars for the luxury car segment. The Tata's therefore were shopping for an opportunity to acquire world class design, development and manufacturing capability for cars in the high end Luxury segment. This when the Fords JLR proposal came up for take over.

Everyone including few executives in Tata's were in for a major surprise when the takeover of the iconic brands of the" JAGUAR & LAND ROVER BRANDS" by the Tata at a very high financial out lay of \$ 2,3 billion towards the acquisition. This the Tata group was definitely not in a position to afford from its own funds and need to borrow, especially in view of it's the huge funds it had raised for the acquisition of CORUS steels by TATA steel for \$ 12.3 billion. There were serious apprehensions and criticisms, from all corners of the world towards this massive merger the Tata's had decided. One could not see any business opportunity for the Tata's at least for the next 10 yrs in view of the huge technological gap between Tata's and the JLR, and that the back ground of the world class Ford Motor company failing to revive JLR in the past 20yrs. There appeared nothing so great in Tata's capability which could be far better than that of the Fords. Besides around this time Tata motors main division the commercial vehicles including the passenger car were accumulating losses in view of the decline in the global automobile markets. However the takeover Deal was concluded in early 2008.

Critical appraisal of the takeover of JLR by TATA Motors:

A) For the Ford motors:

1) The critics felt that Ford Motors is the biggest LOSER in the deal. As against the initial payment of $ 5.0 billion while acquiring the JLR, Ford had spent several billion in its revival efforts for the iconic models of JLR. It had also invested heavily in the R&D infrastructure for new models of Jaguar & Land Rover. As against this it was getting only $1.7 billion from the deal after adjusting for the pension deficit.

2) The business analysts felt that in bargain, Ford was getting a pittance of $1.7 billion was in no way improving the liquidity situation for Ford. They felt that at least by delaying the deal for some more time to recover some of its investments made new products such as the Jaguar XF & LR2 which could have revived the markets for them.

3) With this deal, Ford also will stand to lose the annual royalty payments to the tune of 126 million Pounds from Land Rover all its financial resources. And the losses on Jaguar had eaten away. At the end of the day Ford has got a very Rawdeal

B) For Tata Motors Ltd :

1) The experts feel that this deal is going to hit the finances

of Tata Motors very adversely Besides the bridge loan for 2.3billion,they will need to service an interest burden of $ 30 Million per quarter. This will burgeon in to a steep rise in the annual losses and will definitely affect its market capitalization very severely(Immediately after the takeover deal announcement, Tata Motors shares crumbled down by a massive 6%) The rating agencies also have downgraded the Tata Scripts and moved on to negative implications.

2) Unless there is revival in the market and acceptance of of Jaguar Land Rover brand under Tata Motor's ownership there is not going to be any benefit to the Tatas from this deal. Besides serious quality problems on the Land Rover in compliance to new emission norms which will call for & immediate investments will further drain the financial muscles of Tata's which are already over burdened

3) The design and manufacturing infrastructures at JLR are for quite some time likely to be beyond the reach of Tata's domestic expertise. Excepting for management supervision and pursuing Ford for Continued help in the design& development of new models for Jaguar. Tata's Current core competence will be of little use in the revival attempts for JLR(It is understood that the deal specifies a contract with Ford to continue supplies of Engines for the Jaguar model for 3 more years till JLR has its own capacity increase as required)

People basically disbelieve that what the mighty Fords Could not achieve in 20 years Tatas' with literally no experience in globally acceptable luxury passenger car markets will be able to turn around JLR and make profits for which Ford have burnt their fingers in spite of being one of the great three Auto manufacturers. Hence this deal is likely to be a mill stone around the neck of the Tata Group for a very long time.

Where are the Synergies?

There is a great amount of apprehension in the minds of the experts as also the common man in respect of the synergies between the Indian Tatas' and the iconic JLR. Tatas even today are considered as manufacturers of famous Tata Trucks which occupy major roads in India for goods transport. The common man while appreciating Tata's dare devil entry in the passenger car segment still feels Tatas cannot make world class luxury cars because of their Basic mindset of manufacturing trucks. The very fact that many foreign car manufacturers like the Hyundai,Toyota,Skoda,GM and ,BMW are the leaders in the growing passenger car market(Not to Forget the Indian Maruti Suzuki cars) in the luxury car segment and Tatas are nowhere in this segment gives doubts to feel that one day Tata's Jaguar Cars will be seen on the Indian roads as well.

Even in the Global markets, in spite of the pioneering global marketing expertise of the FORD Motors ,over the past 20 years. Jaguar Cars have failed to attract customers in the biggest markets for luxury cars in US and Asian countries. How could one expect that Tatas' who do not have any representation in the global markets for the luxury passenger cars would be able to penetrate new markets leave alone maintaining same impact as the Fords in the existing markets? On the contrary Tatas' as new owners of JLR are likely to face negative marks on their capability to provide leadership in the marketing & servicing of marquee brands like Jaguar & Land Rover.

Ford Motors excepting for the lower transaction price are going to lose on their royalty income from Land Rover. Besides this deal may work out as a setback since it has failed to resurrect JLR, in spite of heavy investments and new model failures of Jaguar. Besides they are required to settle outstanding pension payments and keep supplying engines to the new owner for 3 more years as per the settlement

The cultural integration between, JLR employees suppliers, customers, and Tatas is one more major issue on which Tats will need to work hard.

The major issues on the technology front are the product Improvement ,new model introduction for the Jaguar and resolution of the serious product quality on the Land Rover models, including compliance to the new emission norms. In general the acquisition deal does not seem to offer many synergy benefits to both the parties post acquisition

The Ambiguities in the deal:

At the time of sealing the deal, the following aspects were not clear,

1. How much and how long will Ford be required to help Tata JLR in servicing and warranty issues on vehicles already on the roads? How long will Ford need to provide technical support to the new owner for the introduction of new models in the pipe line as supply engines for the regular production of Jaguars?

2. How much of the accrued losses of JLR have taken in its books? How big were these amounts? how was the figure of $2.3 billion arrived at since Tata was to take over a near debt free JLR?

3. In a retrospective frame work of recent developments Tatas seem to have been benefitted by the overall recovery in the Global Auto markets, mainly in view of the recovery in the global economic scene. But JLR is likely to be an area calling utmost prudence for a very long time on all fronts for the Tatas. Any turbulence in the markets is likely to throw the situation back to square ONE.

Case Questions:

1. What is the strategic plan both in short and long terms for the TATA's to have invested so heavily in the acquisition of JLR from FORD?

2. Neither TATA's in India nor JLR worldwide are among the top few in the CSI (customer satisfaction Index), in this context, Do you think that TATA's will gain a competitive advantage out of this acquisition?

3. In the view of the heavy investments TATA's has made for acquiring JLR, suggest a business model for recovery of the capital investment.

5. Power OF 10- "Full Throttle"

A VUCA Situation in Two Wheeler segment

Learning Objectives-

The business world has changed dramatically over the last few decades, and we are in a society where change is continuous and it is a fast paced one. So it has become very essential to learn how to manage it as we cannot live without change. Changes are taking place due to technology, new methods adopted in work, changes in thought process of governments, crisis across the globe due to environment or war fears. Global financial market slumps have also added fire to volatility & uncertainty. So in Management it is said VUCA has to be dealt in a suitable manner.

Synopsis:

The case deals with a specific sector in the VUCA (volatility, uncertainty, complexity, and ambiguity) market. The two wheeler segment plays an important role in the Indian economy which was dominated by Bajaj for a very long period. After the domination of Bajaj two wheelers came to an end various players have entered the market where almost a saturation point of the players emerged. So the case deals with this scenario of various players, uncertain as to what shall happen, every manufacturer wanting a foreign technically sound partner and no one knows how customer tastes can vary.

The Case:

Hero has forged an alliance with EBR for high-end bikes and sponsors the EBR team in America's premier motorcycle racing circuit. The 58-year-old big daddy of the world's largest two-wheeler company by volume is gearing up to go global at a time when doubting Thomas's point at dipping domestic sales, predicting an uncertain future for the two-wheeler company. The CEO of a rival company says: "Hero is in a place where Bajaj was many years ago -without a technology partner. The way things are moving in the motorcycles market, it's soon going to be a two-horse race between Honda and Bajaj. Honda on its own is a far more dangerous player than Hero Honda."

In April-October 2012, Hero Moto Corp sold 3.4 million units and registered a negative growth of 1.83% over the same period the previous year. Bajaj Auto too shrank by 4.5% in the same period, while Honda Motorcycles and Scooters India (HMSI) grew by 47%, albeit on a much lower base of 1.5 million units. In the fast growing scooter segment, Hero has a 17% market share, while Honda with 49.3% market share is by far the leader. The contest is rather close between Hero and TVS for the number two position.

What's going on? "When Honda came out with a 100% subsidiary in India (HMSI in 1999), they manufactured only scooters for the first 5 years of their operation since that was the deal with us," says Munjal, echoing how he fended off Honda's challenge in motorbikes long enough for Hero Honda to consolidate and add teeth to volumes. But the hiatus proved a boon for Honda to develop a market for scooters at a time when the segment was sliding. For Hero, it will now indeed be difficult to unseat its established erstwhile partner in a rapidly growing segment.

Another significant shift can be noticed in the traction across the 125cc segment, a sort of aspirational up trading by customers. Traditionally, Hero has championed the 100cc segment and rules the roost with two thirds of the market with winners, such as the Splendor and Passion. "In a full year, Splendor sells about a third of our volumes," claims Dua.

But over the years, Bajaj has built up capabilities in the 125cc space while Hero battles on with three offerings. "Hero's relative advantage will get whittled away as the competition already has credible products in the 125cc space," says a recent report from Citi Group.

Even in the premium segment, Hero's heroics come unstuck. Its market share was down to 7% in August from 24% five quarters ago. Blame it on the slowdown for now, but as the segment continues to grow, Hero may have to bite the bullet from Bajaj (40%marketshare)and Honda (17%)

Nevertheless, it's worth noting that with approximately 70% share in the most popular 100cc segment of the two-wheeler industry, Hero has penetrated deep into the hinterland with almost 5,400 touch points encompassing dealerships, service and spare parts outlets and authorized reps of dealers, while nearest competitor Bajaj stands a distant second with 3,500 touch points. "We will be adding another 400 touch points to our network by the end of this year (taking the total to 5800)," says Anil Dua, Senior Vice President-Sales & Marketing, Hero Moto Corp, when grilled on the Honda challenge.

With the success of the Hero Honda venture behind him, Dua revs up for a repeat performance. "I'm not very concerned about market shares going up and down," he says matter-of-fact, pointing to a newfound vigor post the split with Honda. "I'm looking ahead." In a volume-driven market like India where competition is heating up, despite being market leaders, Hero has stepped up its efforts to go overseas. "We've created an international business division with 16 people as of now and want to grow our international business five times in five years," says Dua. Earlier, Hero Honda had just two people in its overseas division and exported to four countries-Nepal, Sri Lanka, Bangladesh and Colombia-accounting for a mere 3% of its annual turnover. Today, the thinking has changed even though the turning of the tide can take longer.

1. Adding 400 touch points by yearend taking dealership network to 5,800 in FY2012-13

2. Setting up an international business division to scout for global markets and overseas manufacturing potential.

3. Forging alliances with three separate global players in the automotive space - Erik Buell Racing (EBR) of the US for high-end bikes, Austria based AVL for engine technologies and Italian design firm Engines Engineering (EE) for end-toend two-wheeler design solutions.

4. Planned Rs 400 crore investments to set up a fully integrated R&D centre at Kukas, Rajasthan. Built over an area of 250 acre, the center will be the largest two- wheeler R&D set up in the country, which will have over 500 engineers.

5. The company targets US$10 billion in turnover in five years with 10 million unit volumes and 10% of total volumes to come from international business

While unveiling the new brand identity in London O2 Arena last year, Munjal outlined the vision of his company through the Power of 10.

Simply put, in five years, he's eyeing $10 billion in revenues with 10 million units, and at least 10% of the total volumes coming from the international business. Very carefully, the company has recalibrated the nomenclature from 'exports' to 'international business', since it harbors hopes of setting up manufacturing facilities in some of the newer geographies it is venturing into.

"We've appointed distributors in Africa, Central America and Latin America and are first tapping those markets where we believe our products will deliver," claims Munjal in the backdrop of Bajaj Auto's successful foray in the overseas markets, which now forms one-third of its total business by volume.

Changing Scenario

Along with Erik Buell Racing of the USA, Hero has also tied up with AVL of Austria for engine technologies and Italian design firm Engines Engineering (EE) for end-to end two-wheeler design solutions - who are working together to develop the next-generation Hero two wheelers. Hero is reportedly working on several models ranging from low engine displacement to higher powered motorcycles and scooters. However, the first bike on a new platform to hit the market will be a 250cc motorcycle by the third or fourth quarter ofFY2014-15.

Ever since Hero separated from Honda, the company has launched only four products, which could all be termed as Honda's babies in terms of technology. The Honda effect may well continue with a couple of fresh launches in the next fiscal. But does that augur well for the group when the competition has the firepower to deliver more? "In the first 15 years of this company (1985-2000), we launched only six models. From 2001 to 2005, the company launched 15 models. Each year now, companies launch on an average 8-10 models," says Ravi Sud, Senior VP & CFO, Hero Moto Corp. Clearly, Hero falls woefully short of market expectations in the near term.

But the new tie-ups will surely come into force after that and Munjal is upbeat. "The premium segment is currently on the drawing board, well beyond the design board, and we've seen mock-ups and clay models....in 2014, we would have a completely new portfolio." It is learnt that the first bike from Hero will sport a 250cc engine. But skeptics demur as analysts question the effectiveness of the tie-ups, save AVL, a trusted name in engine technologies. "While EBR is a boutique, EE is not a name to reckon with in auto design," says an analyst requesting anonymity. There is also hint of an apprehension of a complete tech overhaul from the existing Japanese platform to the western domain.

Dua dispels that fear. "Instead of completely replacing what our erstwhile partner has done, we need to know about engines, we need inputs on designing and styling, we need to know about racing," he says adding that currently, Hero engineers are working with these partners to "co-develop" the company's future SKU's.

Clearly, the competitors and market watchers know Hero still has a strong franchise and the massive transformation exercise will build a strong platform. "Hero has seen 70 years of evolution under Brij Mohan Munjal. Their understanding of the market is very deep.

The competition can have better technology but that's not sufficient to win the market. Therefore, dislodging the current lead of Hero will be difficult for the competitors," says Ramdeo Agarwal, Jt. MD of Motilal Oswal. "In this very sector, there have been past instances of promoters doing well, in spite of their JV partners walking out. So there is no reason why Hero can't repeat that," adds Ravi Sardana, EVP, and ICICI Securities.

Market watchers say Munjal's chemistry with stakeholders may not be as strong as his father's, Chairman Brij Mohan Munjal, around whom legends of benevolence have been woven. A source even said that once when an employee needed blood, it was Sr. Munjal who came to his rescue by donating his own blood. And the same thread of deep relationships runs through the dealers and distributors as well. Just when CD was interviewing Hero executives Brij Mohan Munjal and his wife passed through the reception of the Hero Moto Corp HQ. A couple of dealers standing at the reception offered him belated Diwali gifts and touched his feet. He blessed them and asked how they were doing, whether they faced any hiccups-all in first name terms.

Conclusions:

However, the larger question is whether Hero will remain

a two wheeler company. "It's about mobility and if Hero Moto Corp is a two wheeler company today, it could be anything tomorrow," says Dua- hinting at larger plays in auto. And he believes that unity of command allows room for such adventures. "It enables you to do visioning, missioning, give a strategic thrust, alignment and then a plan to go for it and execute that plan," he says. With a heat wave as severe as one is witnessing in the two-wheeler category, Hero has a tough battle at hand. The overseas thrust may be one way to battle the crisis but a category leap calls for another round of introspection.

Case Questions:

1. What in your opinion are the possibilities of Hero group maintaining its leadership status with the exit of Honda from its stable?

2. Do you think the Power of Ten strategy feasible? If yes how?

3. With so much of severe competition in the Motor Cycle Market with world known brands like Suzuki, Honda, BMW and many others setting manufacturing facilities in India and Bajaj Auto being a dominant exporter of Motor Cycles supported by its strength with companies such as KTM & BMW- Will Hero Corporation be able to hold its ground and how long?

6. The Pains Of Separation

A Case Study on Organizational Restructuring

Learning objectives

Today businesses and organizations face relentless pressures to become leaner. Such demands are the result of global competition and rapid technology change. Many organizations have responded by corporate restructuring and downsizing, often 'spinning off' divisions originally part of the larger scheme of things. The logic is, when you demerge different units, each unit can focus on specific areas of business, sharply improving their prospects in the larger marketplace. And if the stock prices of the recently demerged entities in the country are anything to go by, the market has definitely given a thumbs-up to most demergers.

Synopsis:

One of the more visible signs of organizational restructuring is that many firms have become flatter on the organizational chart. In search of efficiencies, some of them have removed entire layers of management to speed up communication and reduce head count. But what often ends up roiling the water is the prospect of employee redundancy (HP, which is headed for a split, may cut around 55,000 jobs globally), redeployments and job separation as a company gets into the restructuring mode. A review of literature on spin-offs and demergers seems to suggest that a split in business can be organizationally disruptive as it can cause stress and broken bonds between employees who feel vulnerable and not in control of their careers. Given this, experts suggest corporate leaders must ask some fundamental questions before embarking on a demerger exercise: How can the company work to minimize the human impact of a demerger while remaining competitive? Indeed, how does the psychological contract between the worker and the employer change post a split? Above all, how can the workforce be motivated to perform better after the split?

It must be understood that regardless of whether an organization conceptualizes and designates its spin-off as re- engineering or re-organization of business, the adoption and implementation of workforce reorientation strategies will inexorably produce considerable financial, organizational, and emotional effects. While some such outcomes can be anticipated and are tangible, others have unexpected, long- term consequences that are difficult to measure.

Back to basics

The corporate restructuring exercises (including demergers) have deep psychological scars on employees (existing and the outgoing ones). Casio, who is a professor of Management at the University of Colorado, says that to mitigate the risks companies must begin by asking a simple question: Are we facing a short-term crisis or do we think that our business needs to undergo fundamental structural changes in that we need new plans and new strategy, a complete overhauling to move forward? In other words, to make the move successful, the organization needs to set out the goals clearly before embarking on a demerger - or any other manner of restructuring - exercise. Once the business leader is clear in his mind on what the objective is, the expectation from the employees becomes easier to set. According to Sridhar Ganesan, country head, **Hay Group India**, while the demerger mandate is always clear most of the time - to grow the business in a completely independent landscape - it is the mind shift of employees that needs to be plotted carefully before the restructuring takes place. "Employees can be concerned about their roles in view of the talent movement that will take place.

The accountability of the new company also goes up with the pressure to perform better," he adds.

The best way to deal with this scenario is through communication, crystal clear communication, to be precise. This means the HR has to be taken into confidence early on in the process so that it can chalk out a communication roadmap for the people who stay back, for the people who move on, and for those who must go.

See how **Future Group** managed its demerger exercise. In 2012, Pantaloon Retail India and Future Ventures India decided to demerge their lifestyle fashion businesses into Future Fashion. Given the speed at which the company was restructuring (it further demerged its businesses in fashion, hypermarket and food) even altering its business model time and again, it was natural for the employees to feel uneasy. Looking at the growing restlessness and uncertainty among employees, the company management took two key decisions pretty early on its course-first, that it had to "talk" to the people; and second, that all communication had to flow from one common source that would filter down to the last employee, even those operating from the shop floor.

To this end, the company announced a special-purpose telephone number, dialing which any employee could get in touch with Future Group's founder Kishore Biyani. Additionally, every Friday Biyani addressed and updated the employees on the company's plans. Videos were shot specifically targeting the shop floor staff, in which Biyani briefed his employees about the latest developments at the company. The whole exercise was orchestrated in a manner that people felt they knew what was going on leaving little room for speculation. "We constantly sought feedback from people, tried to understand how we could add value to the employee's role in the restructuring phase," says Kaustubh Sonalkar, head, people office, Future Group.

Planned meticulously over five quarters, the demerger process left very few casualties in its wake. The best part, according to the company, was that there were no lay-offs, zero attrition. "The HR team had so much data that it could distribute roles and job opportunities within the organization," says Sonalkar who agrees that many Indian companies still need to refine the systems and processes to make a demerger smooth. "The spotlight cannot be only on the shareholders; you have to understand that value erosion can happen when employees are dissatisfied or asked to leave," he adds

According to independent HR consultant Gautam Ghosh, "A corporate spin-off is not necessarily bad news for employees. The problem is that many organizations do not communicate a demerger strategy to their employees proactively. In fact, in my experience, even some MNCs, known otherwise for their professional management practices, fail to share a clear roadmap with their country or regional offices making the whole process painful and fraught with risks." Ghosh warns communication that is one-way is not good enough. "A company that runs a global business should consult the leaders of all the countries to assess the HR implications of tough business decisions. This will help them avoid bad press," adds Ghosh.

Analysts say that companies that have split businesses successfully in recent years - such as Marico, Crompton Greaves, Polaris and Wipro - have planned well and have been rewarded handsomely. Some of them have even helped outgoing employees via out-placements with the promise that they can return at an appropriate time in the future.

That said, the communication strategy has to be more refined. Gurpreet Singh, country head, **YSC India**, an HR facilitator, points out that some organizations tend to procrastinate on breaking the news relating to far-reaching changes in the organization by design. "Demergers can create confusion among employees and affect the company's performance at the stock market. Responsible companies must know that it is the employees who have to finally bear the impact of such decisions; some of them may have to pay a heavy price if things go off-track. So it is best if the people know the facts before the shareholders do."

Rajiv Kapoor, chief people officer at **Fortis Healthcare**, adds, "Not informing employees timely about demergers could be a ploy to get rid of some part of the workforce. This includes employees who will start looking for opportunities outside the organization at the sign of trouble. This will ease the downsizing drive."

Clearly then, the success of a business split boils down to transparency and clear conversation between the employer and the employees. The secret sauce is to tick all the boxes relevant for any restructuring exercise: preparing early, putting together a transition team, focusing on clear communication and knowing that engagement (even with outgoing employees) won't be over even after you have gone through the legal routine.

LOOK BEFORE YOU SPLIT

Separation can be painful. When planned carefully, the rewards are huge. Here are six things to think about:

- Use the demerger exercise as an opportunity to address long-term problems. You need to clearly understand why the demerger is taking place after all. Invest time in assessing the impact on those who are moved to the new entity, and the ability of the organization to serve its customers. Answer questions like what systems will be in place for the demerged company? What will be the support from the parent company in the initial phase of operations? What tools will the HR use to communicate with the employees so that the best talent is retained and no one feels shortchanged?

- Before taking a final call on the split, ask employees about their concerns and seek their input. Never underestimate the value of asking your employees for ideas. Even if their ideas do not make good business sense and cannot be put into action, you, as the employer, will have demonstrated to your workers that they matter. Make special efforts to solicit the input of "star" employees or opinion leaders within the organization, for they can help communicate the rationale for the impending restructuring to their fellow employees and promote trust in the restructuring effort. Involve the HR team right at the outset, ask for their inputs in developing the communication that would eventually filter down to employees.

- Keep the channels of communication open while retaining focus on both the employee and the customer. Make employees understand why a new entity is being carved out, or why a division needs to have its own identity instead of being seen as a 'liability'. Explain to customers why a separation from the parent company is important. Communicate in a variety of ways in order to keep everyone abreast of new developments. Executives should be visible, active participants in this process, and be sure that lower- level managers are trained to address the concerns of victims as well as survivors.

- If layoffs are necessary, make decisions in a consistent manner to ensure that employees perceive the process as fair. Before laying off employees, be sure that you have looked at all the options, including asking your employees whether they would be willing to make 'small sacrifices' for the good of the company. Employees can show surprising loyalty and flexibility if they perceive their employer to be fair. Try to retain your best performers, and provide maximum advance notice to employees whose services you need to terminate. Ensure that management at all levels shares the pain and participates in any sacrifices employees are asked to bear.

- Keep the communication going even after the demerger is complete. It could be an idea for HR teams, among other teams, to continue communicating with the people till both the companies achieve stability. This will minimize disturbances to both the parent and the demerged company and reduce speculation.

- Examine all systems and processes in the light of the change of strategy or environment facing the firm. Train employees and their managers in the new ways of operating. There is enough evidence to show that firms in which training budgets are increased following a restructuring are more likely to see improved productivity.

Conclusions

The efforts of larger groups of companies to exit from noncore businesses and spinoff smaller noncore group companies to meet renewed investment demands for core business activity especially due to disruptive changes due to technological changes in terms of globally competitive AI driven product and process lines are creating havoc in the career plans of many executives due to un certainty of their employment as also redundancy of their skillsets. The senior you are more is the risk since you're less amenable to learn and adapt to new skill sets.

Case Questions:

Q1. What should be the strategy for Employees Rehabilitation incase few of them get to be displaced due to organizations demerger or Spinoff strategies?

Q2. What is the proactive strategies to avoid separation due to change in product, process and marketing technology. How do you take care of loyal senior level employees?

Q3. Disruptive Changes are there to stay in every market segment how should the employees work out their career plans since they are likely to be affected by Disruptive changes?

7. Building an Ethical & Smart Organization

Learning Objectives:

All businesses are complex organizational systems that are nested within larger systems, such as national cultures and legal and regulatory systems, and composed of individuals who bring their own values and perspectives to work.

This interplay of personal, organizational and regulatory systems creates a dynamic environment that must be actively managed by leaders to promote the company's long-term success. Ethical failure at any level can bring catastrophe, but achieving good ethics at all levels yields enormous benefits in trust, efficiency and happiness.

Synopsis:

In difficult financial times, companies face various moral issues to try to keep up with their competitors. Although these issues have a direct impact on employee decision making, businesses rarely address how employees should assess the ethics of their actions and incorporate ethics into their decisions. Often this can be alleviated by creating and maintaining a corporate culture with a focus on ethics. Corporate culture is often considered to be both a source of various problems and the basis for solutions and is certainly a factor that determines how people behave in an organization. The role of management in the organizational culture is important as it both acts as a role model for the employees and can also directly influence the behavior and culture to improve organizational performance. Of course there are better methods that management can use to incorporate ethics into the corporate culture or increase the likelihood that its employees will act ethically and these methods are explored.

Introduction

When one evaluates the reasons for the fall of companies such as Enron, Lehman Brothers and WorldCom, what connects the dots is a stupefying disregard for ethics. Closer home, Ranbaxy's recent run- in with the US Food and Drug Administration has invited renewed questions about the governance, compliance and ethics practices of a section of firms in India and indeed across global economies.

While there is no reassurance in stating that incidents like Ranbaxy or Wockhardt or the fact that some of India's best-selling small cars have failed independent crash tests conducted by a global car safety watchdog are aberrations rather than reflections of a systemic problem, misconduct within its own walls remains one of the most lethal threats to any organization. Put in another way, a lack of ethics is like a missed opportunity in a world where competitive advantage is fast becoming a commodity. Says Rita McGrath, a professor at Columbia Business School, and author of The End of Competitive Advantage, "Companies can build advantages on the basis of ethics. High ethical standards tend to be correlated with other positive attributes such as attention to quality, fair dealings with people and transparency that can give organizations an advantage." Needless to say, the benefits of good corporate governance and a culture of ethics percolate down to all levels of stakeholders —investors and top- quality employees are attracted to ethical companies.

Given that, what are the challenges that prevent companies from embracing and — more importantly — sustaining a culture of ethics and good conduct? What are the ways in which companies can ensure they don't stray from their intent at the time of establishment? And what is the best way to react if a situation involving an ethical transgression does arise?

Ethical Corporate Culture

In his book The Tipping Point, Malcolm Gladwell has spoken about the ' Broken Windows' theory that draws from the field of criminology. It states that crime tends to increase in situations where the atmosphere reflects that 'anything goes'. If a broken window is not repaired, it somehow gives a message that it is okay to break more windows. The norm applies in the corporate setting too.

Integrity, which is one of the core values of any organization, should be held above all other forms of behavior. "At the heart of an ethical culture are the shared values and assumptions of the people in the organization. These provide the overall direction for the behavior of employees," says Mona Cheriyan, Director, human resources, ASK Group.

"A strict enforcement of codes of compliance and a culture of zero intolerance for malpractices and frauds deter any probable ethical lapses," adds Abhay Gupte, senior director, Deloitte.

Having said that, it is difficult for a company to decide and craft an ethical corporate culture somewhere down its journey. It has to be done right at the beginning. " It should be in the DNA of the promoters and leaders, and must be part of everything that the company does from day one," says Narayan PS, vice-president and head, sustainability, Wipro.

While we know that senior leaders set the tone for action, they do not by themselves achieve the outcome for the organisation. It is how leaders act to promote right action that determines the performance and the culture. "While ethical codes may vary from company to company, the basic fabric remains the same," says DilepMisra, president and head corporate human resources, JK Tier.

At all times, management must take cognizance of staff

turnover and grievances, customer complaints, product defects and returned items, expressed dissatisfaction of contractors and suppliers, cases of litigation triggered by unethical behavior, and community unhappiness with corporate behavior as reflected by media reports, citizen protests etc. "The prevailing environment in society is so poor and corruption is so widespread, that creating an oasis of ethics is challenging. The only way out is that the tone has to be set at the top, else ethics will just be lip service," says Ravi Venkatesan, author and former chairman, Microsoft India.

Ethics also includes placing the organization's interest before the promoter's interest. " For instance, the employment of a promoter's son should be driven on merit and not on anything else," says Harish Mariwala, chairman & MD, Marico.

Often those integrity failures are a result of senior individuals crossing ethical boundaries. " In a hurry to reach to the top and to beat competition, they compromise on ethics," says author and leadership guru Ms. Rao One must note that having a culture of ethics and compliance in a corporation is not a guarantee that there will not be breaches. What saves a company is the swiftness with which it redresses its wound.

Formal elements of Ethical Culture

The Tata Group, known for its high 'trust' quotient, believes creating an ethical culture is a journey " from compliance to commitment to consciousness". "It is not a question of the number of rules, but embedding desired values in each employee's consciousness, so that ethical conduct is a spontaneous output," says Mukund Rajan, member, group executive council and chief ethics officer, Tata Sons.

To make core values explicit, and to demonstrate how they translate into behavior in the daily business, an organization should establish formal norms, including codes of conduct, and guidelines and these should be led from the top, says Cheriyan of ASK Group.

Some prerequisites can help a corporation foster ethics in its DNA: there should be clearly enunciated policies, a basic code of conduct, regular communication with employees and a swift investigation system in case of reported malpractices. Here the perspective and role of corporate boards of directors in overseeing ethics and compliance matters within their firms cannot be underestimated.

The Board could also insist on a compliance certificate every quarter, and this certificate ought to be vetted by the audit committee. In fact, audits are good detection mechanisms to keep a tight leash on transgressions — a type of consequence management. In simple words, audits form the execution part of an ethical culture. While internal audits help create a culture of ethics, external audits give out a message to outsiders about the internal culture of ethics. "The Board must mete out punishment, including sacking the CEO if he is found guilty," says TVMohandas Pai, chairman, Manipal

Global Education Services, and an ex Infosys hand. "Once the punishment is certain, the culture is firmed up." That is the easier part, the benefits of which have been well documented. What is critical is to understand that ethics is different from compliance. The latter is the straightforward 'rules and regulations' part of ethics, and doesn't require high education. Ethics is a larger universe that goes beyond just following the law, and therefore, reflects how a company is oriented. It is possible for a company to be legally compliant and yet not have a strong culture of ethics.

The process of creating a culture of ethics probably starts from the process of recruitment. While hiring a person, it is not enough to assess only his/ her professional and technical competencies. It is equally important to look at the fit with the values of integrity and ethics. Here's how Wipro does it: its employees — campus and lateral hires — are inducted into Wipro's ethics journey at the very start of their association with the company. Thereafter, mandatory annual test and certification process, leadership training sessions, electronic mailers, posters etc constantly guide employees to follow the Wipro Code of Business Conduct (COBC). Any breach of COBC, identified from concerns raised through Wipro's ombuds process, is handled swiftly and with seriousness, reveals Padmanabhan A, similar plane, the Board at JK Corporation meets every quarter to check on compliance breaches.

Challenges for Sustaining an Ethical Culture

But sustaining an ethical culture doesn't come without its challenges. It is particularly difficult to create and sustain this culture in a dispersed global organization. First, you have to define the culture and create a shared meaning of ethics across the organization. For instance, a media house may prohibit giving or receiving gifts, which could be an ethical guideline. But in India, gifting is accepted as part of culture, so a guideline like that could go against the popular wisdom, which poses a challenge.

Second, how do you propagate the non- negotiable? "If you define many things under ethics, the education challenge in the company is high," says Santrupt Misra, CEO, Carbon Black Business and group HR director, Aditya Birla Group. But the real moment of truth is how a company reacts to the ethical crisis. Does it wait for someone to point it out or accept it publicly and make corrections proactively? Or worse — does it play the blame game? That apart, ambitious Indian company wanting to play the global field must bear in mind that often, norms of the West may be more stringent than the ones back home. Critical lapses may not be overlooked so easily, as the case of Ranbaxy demonstrates. This is also a shift from the experiences of the past, when expectations from Indian companies were low.

"It is now important for corporate India to match up to global standards," says Mariwala.

A handful of companies The Strategist spoke to argued if they were to comply with all the innumerable laws, it will slow processes down. "But in the long run, look at the damage you will do to your own reputation and brand salience if you don't comply. You will have a longer ground to cover," says Rajeev Dubey, president, group HR, corporate services and aftermarket, Mahindra & Mahindra. "At the end of the day, good reputation means good business. And reputation can't be outsourced."

SMART Ranbaxy's recent run- in with the US Food and Drug Administration has invited renewed questions about how to strengthen compliance mechanisms and ethical leadership within firms.

Conclusion:

Ethical issues have posed major challenges to companies in recent years and there will undoubtedly be more in the future. Good ethical practices may not be easy to maintain. However, with a well-designed ethics policy, ethical leadership and implementing ethics into organizational strategies and processes, it will make it easier. The reason is because these factors are incorporated into the organizational culture. How might a culture of character be developed? It is certainly by intention. It is the responsibility of particular individuals within the organization, i.e. Its leadership. Strong leaders model and pass on ethical aspects of the culture and use techniques like structure, decision-making processes, rewards, norms, heroes, stories, rituals and other artifacts to create a strong culture. This is the foundation for creating a culture of character, where members of the organization "know what is right, value what is right, and do what is right."

In all cases, management must be committed to ethical conduct. To conclude, despite the economic crisis, there are clear and long-lasting advantages of establishing an ethical culture. With a more open and ethical organizational culture, the more positively employees tend to commit to corporate social responsibility and this will generate more honest environments. As a consequence, this may not only reduce the unhealthy environment that began the financial crisis, but will also help in restoring the health of the financial system that caused it

Case Questions:

Q1. Are workers at all levels encouraged to take responsibility for the consequences of their behavior? To question authority when they are asked to do something that they consider to be wrong? How?

Q2. What is your overall evaluation of the organizations ethical culture? What are its areas of strength and weakness?

Q3. Does a formal code of ethics and/ or values exist? Is it distributed? How widely is it used? Is it reinforced in other formal systems, such as reward and decision making systems?

8. The enlightened 'Employee Unions'

A case study of negotiating with knowledge workers and their unions

Learning objectives:

- To identify the advent of Internet Technology and the globalised markets.

- To discuss about the commitment to cost, quality and time, that have been the most essential factors to ensure business survival.

- To understand their roles & responsibilities, correctly and effectively towards a common objective of continuing to be in Business.

- To identify the IT implosion in all aspects of business management.

- To find a paradigm shift in the approach to negotiations between the employer and the employees.

- To discuss about the current state of peaceful and productive employee relations(ER)

Synopsis:

The IT implosion in all aspects of business management also have demanded appropriate levels of education and training in the skills required for at all levels of an organization. Today everyone from the gate security to the salesmen is required to be computer literate to be able to manage their day to day organizational roles. Every workman (Sorry, They need to be addressed as 'Associates') in today's situation needs to be able to handle operations which are in majority of cases computer controlled. In general this has led to an overall improvement of the educational levels at all business processes and also in understanding, the parameters which decide the business survival.

The Case Contents

The Employee unions and their leaders are no exception to this trend. Over a period of previous one decade we normally do not hear of violent labor disturbances and slogan mongering and red flag demonstrations in the major Industrial Estates across India. There appears to be a sea change in the attitude and approach to employee related negotiations which are done across the table or on a continuous basis between the affected parties, using all modern methods of communications such as presentations, deliberations involving members of the parties to the negotiations on equal footing, trying to understand each other's viewpoints more constructively and in the long term interests of organization.

This case study attempts to focus on the above and look for sustainability issues of this paradigm change and seeks the participants valued comments on the perpetuity of the current state of peaceful and productive employee relations(ER)

Few Examples of Educated Unionism:

1. The garment and allied workers union-(gawu):

This union covers is a recognized Employee union of the garment workers largely from Gurgaon-Manesar- Bhiwandi belt. One of the Major units in this belt is the VIVA Global the main suppliers of readymade garments Marks & Spencer's.

The major issue related the working conditions for the labor force in the manufacturing setup due to extremely hot ambient temperatures and lack of drinking water facilities. What is important to be noted is that the union leader of GAWU is Mrs. Ananya Bhattacharjee, who is a computer science degree holder from the Texas University and has worked in global software giants in the Silicon Valley in the US. Mrs. Ananya Bhattacharjee (A lady in her Fifties) is driven by her conviction that she needs to resolve the problems faced by the workmen due to high handedness of the respective management. She believed that in order to achieve her deeper intentions of fighting against injustice on the down trodden that, she has to be with the society where such exploitations happen.

Mrs .Ananya was able to pick up all the serious issues of the Garment workers at VIVA Global, and through her concerted efforts and extensive use of internet based communications, was able to get VIVA black listed from the buyers community but also got the Global attention drawn towards the plight of the workers through effective internet campaigning and collective bargaining. VIVA management while rectifying the maladies of the Workmen realized the writing on the wall that they need to be proactive in resolving issues of the workmen and treat them their feelings with due respect and empathy. On a similar footing Mrs. Ananya also got the issues at the WALMART operations to get the equivalent floor level wages for its employees in its Indian operations.

Today GAWU has nearly 3000 workmen as its members. Today the Industrial belt has lots of harmony and positively oriented Industrial Relations climate. All this has been possible due to professional approach inculcated by the union leader in most of the Units and making the Managements conscious of their responsibilities.

2. Maruti suzuki employees union:

Most of us aware of the recent labor unrest in the Manesar plants of MSUL. But what is seen as an eye opener is that the workers union is exhibiting leadership and organizational skills of higher degree rather than slogan mongering or violent protests or militancy.

One more thing which is highly perceptible is the coming together and working together of nearly 11 unions in the area and conducting meetings to reengineer their tactics to rally the total unorganized sector and voice their demands on a common plat form. In the common meetings of union leaders they even discuss issues such as general price rise due to inflation, various disinvestment strategies adopted by scrupulous managements, and other industry specific issues from long term points of interests for the members of the unions.

One more important aspect which needs to be noted is that these union leaders would not like to involve any political leader in their efforts get their issues resolved. They express the feeling that 'Politics without dynamic grass roots experience is a corrupt politicization of Labor issues'.

3. Honda motorcycles & scooters India (HMSI)):

The union at HMSI is led by an internal union which proudly claims that they have been able to weed out all the past misunderstandings and now they involve themselves in to resolving even the issues faced by the management in the smooth running of the operations.

A glaring example of such an initiative by the union at HMSI to help the management in resolving the Managements issue was its participation in the meeting with the vendors of the company in making them to agree to shift their base of operations from Haryana to Rajasthan, where HMSI is to establish a new factory which the vendors were refusing with the management reps.

4. Toyota Kirloskar employees union:

The Employee union at the Toyota Kirloskar plant near

Bangaluru in Karnataka recently introduced a new productivity increase proposal by the Management. On the same issue there was likely to a violent strike by the union, since they felt that the management was using pressure tactics and keeping the union in dark about the process to be followed for achieving the targeted productivity increase.

But wiser counsels prevailing the management decided to make a detailed presentation to the union on the issue of productivity increase and allowed the union to testify the new process through seeking professional guidance from outside. This resulted in an amicable settlement between the management and the union.

The union leader said: 'Earlier the management's stance was hostile and it did not want to discuss anything with the workers, but they realized that the strikes are self defeating and cause loss of production. Now members of the management team even agree to correct their mistakes during negotiations.'

Mr. Tapansen, MP and General secretary of CITU says "In 90%companies today, the workers want increase in productivity, because they get better incentives that way" this indicates a marked difference and departure from tester years when the workers vehemently opposed any move by the ,management to demand increased productivity.

It is a common scene now a day that during productivity and wage negotiations the union leaders extensively use laptops and presentations. And substantiate their stand by providing global data on compensations Vs productivity. It is also seen that in quite few cases there are MBA degree holders amongst the union representatives

In fact recently a delegation from German union Leaders visited to study the strategy followed by unions in Indian operations which enable smooth negotiations between the management and the workers union without any strikes or violence.

The Case of UNITES a Bangalore based union representing the IT/ITES employees led by the union leader who was till recently a team leader in a call center job, with nearly 18000 members from 500 companies, is the largest readdress body for It employees in India. The Union regularly conducts web based campaigns, emails and over social media including Face Book and Twitter. The union committee meets every two months locally and once a year nationally. The union has successfully thwarted attempts by few foreign companies shift their base from India to other Locations resulting in mass retrenchment and prevailed on the managements to reverse their decisions.

It appears from the International Labor union scenario that they have delinked from any political affiliations. In the UK and Us there are powerful unions negotiating with individual employers without any political clout. The same is seen across European countries and even in Japan. The Role of the Unions has become more focused on negotiations with the employers rather than dealing through political contacts.

The outcome:

Due to professional approach of Ms. Ananya, serious issues running into the manufacturing belt was raised on digital platforms. Due to professional approach inculcated by the union leader in most of the Units and making the Managements conscious of their responsibilities.

Highly educated union leaders proved excellent style of leadership and organization skills helped in resolving various issues on a common platform, and resolving the issues without any political leader's involvement. They express the feeling that

'Politics without dynamic grass roots experience is a corrupt politicization of Labor issues'.

The tactics of involving the operations and management to resolve managerial issues and misunderstanding helped in smooth running of production and operations.

Emerging technologies has brought a drastic change to solve disputes between the management and the workers union without any strikes and violence. With the help of presentations management was able to explain the cause loss of productivity.

Future scenario

Educated union leaders would help in the increase of future production. Educated union leaders would play a major role in resolving employee disputes and negotiations.

Technology and social platforms would be the latest trend to voice out internal issues, which may lead into the defaming activity of the organization. Tech savvy leaders can be the best strategies in understanding the market trends, economic situations and national and international business environment.

Conclusions:

The union has successfully thwarted attempts by few foreign companies shift their base from India to other Locations resulting in mass retrenchment and prevailed on the managements to reverse their such decisions.

It appears from the International Labor union scenario that they have delinked from any political affiliations. In the UK and Us there are powerful unions negotiating with individual employers without any political clout. The same is seen across European countries and even in Japan. The Role of the Unions has become more focused on negotiations with the employers rather than dealing through political contacts.

Case questions:

1. Do you think the scenario as explained in the above case is a reality and is there to stay hereafter for major Industrial estates across the Country?

2. What strategy do you suggest could be adopted by major Industry blocks in the country to establish a very long term peaceful IR in spite of volatile market and economic situations at the national; & International Business environments.

3. With the Individual Union Leaders having expertise in the business processes the role of government in IR management seems to be becoming irrelevant, do you think it is good for the unions and the employers in the long term?

9. Leveraging China

A Case Study on Strategic Leveraging

Learning objectives:

Study of Micromax's strategy of rebadging the handset and sailing them in the India market is important. Not only this the way the Micromax did the research of Indian consumers demands is interesting in this. Also In 2011, Micromax shipped four million handsets worldwide in the second quarter. It's cornered 8 per cent share in the home market, it's growth to 48 per cent annually and continued selling 1.5 million phones every month in most of the countries, is very challenging to do study on it. The another objective is to study the how and why phone market in India was pretty much a seller's market. The another objective is to study how it penetrated to Indian market by launching a phone with a 30-day power backup which was the necessity of Indian customers. It is also important to study how Micromax has given affordable handset price.

Synopsis:

The simple strategy applied by the Micromax was, create high volumes, reach the customer base through effective distribution, give them products that are innovative and cost-effective. The Apple and Samsung lagged behind due to affordable handset price compared to Micromax with same features. Micromax launched handset as per their necessity of Indian market like 30-day power backup.Micromax orders 5,00,000 handsets at the entry level from their contract manufacturers in China at one go. The orders 5,00,000 handsets volume is a example of growth in turn over and better cost. The appreciable thing of Micromax was it worked hard for securing sound and formidable partnerships, especially with the chipset manufacturers.

The Case :

The history of Micromax(2011-12 revenue: Rs 1,978 crore), which ventured into the mobile phone market in 2008, is one of the most fascinating success stories in the Indian consumer electronics industry. In barely five years, the company has come to occupy the third position (by volume) in the mobile handset market in India and is at No. 12 globally. It leads the Indian tablet market with a share of 18.4 per cent, ahead of veterans Samsung and Apple. The Gurgaon-headquartered company owes its success not just to the ticket it puts on its products or the speed with which it puts new designs on the shelves but to how it has managed these two crucial product inputs by leveraging China. To be more specific, the labour cost advantage and the production flexibility that China offered.

Big deal, you may say, given that almost every other handset brand in the world manufactures its products in China. Right from the Apples to the Samsungs to many of our home-grown brands like Karbonn, a whole host of players reaped China's arbitrage advantage.

But here is the stumper: the strategy that offered Micromax its biggest advantage in its first five years is under threat and it will require a re-examination by the company — and a number of other multinationals with Chinese production — of their overall supply-chain strategies.

The reason is simple. At Shenzhen, where some of China's largest electronics manufacturers are located, the minimum wage is set for a 13.3 per cent hike from this year — a move that could have a ripple effect across the world's major technology companies. According to some estimates, between 2005 and 2010, basic manufacturing wages in the country have soared roughly 70 per cent. "Eventually, Indian companies sourcing products and components from China need to develop local infrastructure. The reports of underage laborers and inhumane work conditions at some Chinese factories can have a cascading effect on the reputation of brands that source from China," says a telecom expert.

What has made Micromax's life a little more complicated is its recent entry into categories like tablets and LED TVs. In short, if you were to add the increasing cost of monitoring suppliers and of compliance, that labour cost advantage Micromax enjoyed when it started out looks even more precarious.

To understand what Micromax needs to do here on, we need to first understand how the company harnessed China to reach the Top 5 bracket in the Indian mobile phone market. In an earlier interview , Rahul Sharma, co-founder, Micromax, had said: "The strategy is simple: create high volumes, reach the customer base through effective distribution, give them products that are innovative and cost-effective. Finally, create a strong brand." Micromax's strategy of associating with Bollywood and cricket has also helped. The company's advertising and marketing spend last year, according to experts, was to the tune of Rs 150 crore, which would be roughly what Britannia or Heinz spent on their brand communication that year.

What has also set Micromax apart is the speed at which it has been able to put products in the market and its tremendous reach. According to MritunjayKapur, country MD, Protiviti, the world's largest independent business and risk consulting firm, "Players like Micromax are constantly pushing the product profile — they have been able to identify their markets well and be where the customer is." So, where Micromax takes barely a month or two to launch products, another big international brand requires roughly 18 months for a similar product to go through the retail pipeline.

In effect, Micromax's growth strategy has followed three clear stages, explains an industry insider. When it started out, the company picked handsets from China, rebadged them and sold them in the India market. In the second stage, it realised the need to do extensive research in terms of Indian consumers' demands and product development. Now it has crossed over into a new phase, where the company has started following a mix-and- match strategy — getting some products manufactured in China and other countries, sourcing components from abroad and manufacturing some of the newer lines in India.

In a way, the changes in Micromax's growth strategy have followed the evolution of the mobile consumer in India. When it started its journey in 2008, the mobile phone market in India was pretty much a sellers' market. "Consumers were adapting to what was being offered," Micromax's Sharma says "We worked the other way round, trying to understand what the consumer's needs really were." This focus on the consumer led to the launch of its first product — a phone with a 30-day power backup. "People in Indian villages needed mobile handsets with enormous battery backup given the precarious electricity situation," explained Sharma.

According to Anshul Gupta, principal research analyst, Gartner, a technology research firm, by getting products manufactured in China, Micromax could offer products at a price about 40 per cent less than what other global players were offering. "An Apple or a Samsung, which were also getting their products manufactured in China, would demand a mark-up based on the brand value; for a newcomer like Micromax that was never an issue. So they could offer similar features at a lower price," says an industry hand.

"The basic strategy of Micromax has been 'Affordable Innovation'," says an ex-employee of Micromax. In his view, the strategy at Micromax has always been clear: to look at four critical components of a phone which also determine its price. These include the screen, the camera, the chipset and the memory used in the device. It's here that the cost of each model of handsets is determined. Deepak Mehrotra, chief executive officer at Micromax, says the company is driven by what customers want. So, the cost is also determined to what the consumer back home expects. "So, if my target consumer doesn't particularly require a great camera feature, instead of giving a 8 megapixel camera, our handset will have a 5 megapixel one, which will obviously bring the price down," explains Mehrotra.

"Pick up a box (of a mobile handset from any company) and you will see most are produced in China. The country clearly has built economies of scale and knows how to play it right. Why just us, manufacturing across categories is done in China, thanks to the cost efficiencies, eco-system and how they come together," says Mehrotra.

Though Micromax didn't create 'reference designs' initially — preferring to simply give instructions to its third-party manufacturers in China — its' winning strategy was to quickly start its R&D facility, create prototypes and instruct contract manufacturers on what the company expected.

"The real clincher for Micromax was in identifying the Tier I rung of manufacturers, and then getting those manufacturers to work on our specifications, our innovations," added the former Micromax employee. Right at the outset, Micromax took pains to mark out those manufacturers in China who were working with global brands. Fox Conn, the world's largest contract manufacturer, for instance, has been associated with Apple products, according to the employee. BYD, similarly, has been associated with Nokia production and also works on Micromax's handsets, he adds, saying that the company never bothered with the Tier II or the Tier III manufacturers where inferior quality of chipsets etc are used.

"For us, it was always the top tier of manufacturers — those who worked for the Apples and the Samsungs of the world that had to design our products too," says this executive, adding that typically Micromax orders 5,00,000 handsets at the entry level from their contract manufacturers in China at one go. The volume growth in turn ensures better cost efficiencies. In 2011, for instance, Micromax shipped four million handsets worldwide in the second quarter. It cornered 8 per cent share in the home market, grew 48 per cent annually and continues selling roughly 1.5 million phones every month in most of the countries that it operates in.

Besides leveraging the cost effectiveness of China (Tier I manufacturers in China can typically charge $17 upwards per handset) says the ex-employee of Micromax, the company has worked hard at securing sound and formidable partnerships, especially with the chipset manufacturers.

On a new wicket

Micromax's focus these days on is building its manufacturing infrastructure in India. "It is a consumer durables company diversifying into other categories," says Gupta of Gartner. Micromax's facility in Himachal Pradesh already manufactures television sets and some tablet models.

"Micromax now cannot afford to be just another 'Fringe Player' that manufactures products in China and sells them in India," says Kumar Kandaswami, senior director, Deloitte in India. "Eventually, India needs to script a 'China' story in terms of manufacturing its products at home," he adds.

The reason is obvious: China is losing the advantage of labor cost arbitrage, a reason why even companies like Apple and GE have decided to decided to shift product lines from China. "Because Chinese wages are rising rapidly," says an analyst, "it makes sense to return manufacturing of a wide range of goods, with moderate levels of labor content and high logistics costs, to India." Re-shoring may also make particular sense for bulky goods, like television sets, which naturally incur higher transportation costs. "There are many hidden factors involved in sourcing heavy appliances from outside suppliers," says a senior marketing executive with an appliances company. "These variables include greater supply chain complexity, longer cycle times, quality issues and responsiveness to local demand. A local supply chain makes it easier for a company with a wide portfolio to respond to any sudden supply chain disruption or other unpredictable event."

Not everyone thinks the China story is over though. Amitava Chattopadhyay, INSEAD Chair Professor in marketing and innovation, for example, says, "China is a cheap manufacturing base for almost anything — toys, cars, electronics." so, work will continue to happen in China.

But global players are setting up and growing their own facilities or scouting for opportunities in countries such as Vietnam, Indonesia and Cambodia to have greater control over cost and quality. "Wherever you get economies of scale, it is good. It could be in China, Taiwan, or elsewhere," says Mehrotra.

Ultimately, analysts believe that the correct balance can be struck through careful planning. And while Micromax grapples with supply chain issues, what works in its favor is that it is no longer a single product company and faces dilemmas that many other brands confront.

Conclusion:

China is a cheap manufacturing base for almost anything — toys, cars, electronics- and hence handset's chip too. So Micromax focused on securing sound and formidable partnerships with the cheap manufacturing companies and launched rebadged handsets at affordable price to Indian market. The Company also studied the requirement of Indian customer and released products accordingly. That is the reason Micromax could able to create high volumes, and reach the customer base through effective distribution. Ultimately Apple and Samsung were has to lag behind in the sales. The big volume order of 5,00,000 handsets is the evidence to this, and it so ensured the growth in turn over too.It is Leverage by the strategies adopted by them.

Case Questions:

1. Do you think that the Growth Strategy(Leveraging China) Micromax is sustainable in the long Run??

2. How should Indian economist/strategists respond to such a cross country leveraging which is likely to drain business potential in the host country(India)??

3. In an economic situation being precarious more so in India with its political nuances how could one steer clear of possible business issues at both ends ie Chinas raising labor costs and India's inability to fresh investments in industrial sectors?

10. The Directors and the In directors

A case study in 'corporate governance'

Learning objectives:

1. To analyse the need for the concept of corporate governance

2. To assess the impact of globalization on business ethics

3. To evaluate the association between the degree of material comfort attained by mankind and the tendency to blatantly flout norms.

Synopsis:

Over the previous few years we have been hearing about the issues in 'Corporate Governance' (CG) in the corporate circles and through the claims at the various industry associations such as the CII,ASSOCHAM, FICCI and few others. To a common man who has a very superficial understanding about the happenings in Indian business scenario, this appears to be yet another jargon meant for the publicity purposes of the concerned business units to attract the attention of the commoner to indicate that they are up to incorporating some altogether new techniques of business management through which their superiority over the others in competition needs to be differentiated. But the 'Aamadmi' is not able to locate even a distant indication of any improvements at the market place due to these claims of corporate governance and the 'bla–bla ' that happens at the board meetings . For him the things have moved from bad to worse in the products & services he was used to so far. The big malls and multiplexes have taken away the personal contacts, credit terms and the affordable prices and near home locations he was used to till recently.

Corporate Governance: a utopian concept?

Corporate Governance in India is a comparatively new concept (not necessarily new in its philosophy & ground rules). As a sequel to liberalization and globalization of the Indian Economy, all the concerned were exposed to the global requirements of ethical and legal ways of conducting business internationally. Initially the government did appoint various committees of well known business leaders such as the committee headed by Mr. Rahul Bajaj, Mr. Kumarmangalam Birla, Mr. Narayan Murthy of Infosys. Subsequently, the company law board, and SEBI have provided guide lines in the form of definite sections of the CLB & Listing Norms, etc for evaluating and certifying the corporations' eligibility to carryout businesses in India and abroad. In case of mergers and acquisitions the Competition Committee looks into the compliance aspects to provide support and protections to the stake holders in the business. Many organizations of course have adopted more stringent CG norms in their business practices to ensure compliance to the ethical and legally permissible operating practices in the conduct of their businesses. In order to ensure protection of the stakeholders interests, further rules have been made in the CG compliance norms, the important ones being the appointment of Independent Directors on the Boards of every listed company to monitor & control the greedy and sometimes illegal interests of the promoters for short term gains, disregarding the long term interests of the business and its stakeholders. CLB also recommends institution of various committees at the board and CEO levels of the companies to keep a constant watch on the various business transactions of the organizations including the remunerations paid to the senior level executives. The role of the Independent Directors are made more specific and are held responsible for oversight in the major business decisions made by the organization on which they are appointed as Independent Directors. The role of the IDs (Independent Directors) is considered as comparable to and sometimes exceeding that of the external auditors of the company. The details of the credentials of the IDs are to be disclosed in the annual meetings of the shareholders and the appointments are to be approved by the shareholders. There is also a requirement that the remunerations paid to each of the IDs be included in the annual statement of accounts along with compliance report on the other norms of CG. This is one of the reasons that the Annual Reports of various companies have become thicker in the recent years. The CG norms are also supposed to reflect the CSR initiatives of the organizations towards the society in which they operate as responsibilities towards its stakeholders. The annual reports also dwell in details about the various CSR projects under taken by the companies. It is however to be noted that CSR activities of the major Indian Corporations such as the Tatas, Bajaj, and Birlas were more pronounced much before the CG initiatives in the globalised Indian business. In fact, there appears to be a lull in such initiatives post globalization due to CG compliance requirements which perhaps have put certain constraints on thefree-will initiatives towards CSR of these setups.

Does spelling out CG norms necessarily build trust?

'Corporate governance' even for the educated class, appears like yet another exercise in vein like the ISO 9000, BS 9000certification norms which had only very short term impact in the last decade. As on today no one seems to bother about these norms of product and service quality amidst the rush of the 'Buy one get two free' labels which multiply the quality and performance issues(problems) of the same brand products of which the customers were more satisfied in their original 'Sons Ltd &Bros Ltd' shops &services. Popular brands such as Bajaj, Tata, Mafatlal, Park Avenue, Brook Bond, Colgate, etc., never needed in the past any such false incentives for promoting product sales and services at the markets. But as on today we are not sure if the same can be said about these very and other new players in spite of their compliance to the famous ISO,BS certificates and now with a new cap of compliance to the Corporate Governance norms. The basic TRUST in the consistent quality and service standards seems to have been vitiated amidst claims of globalization & world class standards. Even the respective company managements and the members of their boards often do not seem to agree with the correct interpretation and understanding of what good corporate governance implies. In the most simple terminology 'Corporate Governance' refers to the commitment of the organization to carry out its normal and regular business, in the appropriate, legal, ethical and transparent manner. Many however are confused in the correlation of this simple definition, and use the provisions of the guide lines to attract investors, and customers by producing volumes of write ups in the company balance sheets, in the most glamorous words and styles of presentation towards compliance to corporate governance norms. In fact it is a misnomer to term these as norms since there are no legally binding, effective, and evaluative norms on CG. Even at the global level there are more loop holes in the CG norms than the norms themselves. The recent episodes of Lehman Brothers, Enron, Goldman Sachs, not to forget Satyam of the Indian fame, the spicy events of the IPL, and the yet to unwind CWG are glaring instances of the loop holes being much wider and bigger than the provisions of CG and any other National or International legal and ethical norms of business. While teaching the topics on Business Ethics and morale, the concerned faculty necessarily quote the high sounding and glamorized 'Vision, Mission and Objectives' statements of major organizations in India and abroad to the students in management studies. Every faculty nowadays faces embarrassing situations, since the same companies are frequently caught on the wrong side of law of which once they had referred as ideal or model examples of great organizations, noted for their commitment to ethical and legally transparent ways of conducting business. It becomes necessary for the faculty to give unbelievable excuses to ward off such distortions in the business related behaviors of reputed companies to try to remove doubts and confusions in the minds young students. As on today there will be more case studies on business failures due to the scandals rather than any sustainable success stories.

Reality bites

The issue in this case is basically questioning the impact of compliance requirements of the Corporate Governance and similar initiatives of the globalised economies. The instances of extreme contrasts between on paper claims of renowned companies. If we take a single example of Satyam Computers, we find that the Satyam Management was adjudged as the Indian company which has acquired global glory, mainly on account of its fair and highly ethical ways of doing business along with its major contribution in the form of major CSR initiatives.

There were expert committees to evaluate Satyam for such National and International level Awards. All these committees were required to physically verify the status of compliance of CG & CSR initiatives at Satyam before bestowing the laurels. Within 24 hrs after the chief architect of Satyam Mr Ramlingam Raju on the 7th Jan 2009 announced about the financial irregularities in Satyam, the entire world cried foul and declared Satyam as the worst scandalized company on the globe.

The basic questions to an intriguing mind are what tempted Satyam to undertake the down trodden path of fraud and deceit, in its otherwise enviable record as the best managed company? Could the compulsory requirements of the global capability index such as credibility status in business terms and the formality of submission of documents to claim compliance to the global CG norms as eligibility criteria, etc. lead to maneuver the scandalous initiatives to create a mask of **excellence** in the company's credentials?

How could a very small group of Satyam Family members along with few of their senior level executives, and alleged role of the external financial consultants of world repute, manage to put an extremely opaque screen against exposition of the highly objectionable acts of fraud and deceit committed by the top management of the Company? Similarly the fraudulent, scandalous deals and activities of the ENRONs of the world, the unceremonious down fall of the Lehman Brothers in the US, the Madoff misadventures are they in any way less serious than the drug mafias of the world over? One claims to be sane and reliable whereas the other declares his business as unsavory, but the net objectivity is not far different, is it ?

The Somalian pirates have made exploitation of the rich through brutal acts of kidnapping and high jacking the merchant ships for their basic needs of food and drugs, but it is limited to a particular area of activity, where as the misdeeds of many world leaders in business have serious repercussions on the global economy, leading to catastrophic consequences. The acrimonious scenes we encounter in the political environment of most of the countries, the other scandals in high society lives of the glamour world in spite of   global prescriptions   on codes of conduct and ethical behavior including the **Corporate Governance** requirements in all walks of life are issues in ensuring a reliable and sustainable economic progress and world order seem like chasing a mirage.

Conclusions:

We cannot deny the fact that today we are better informed, scientifically and technically better prepared and provided with security and safety against major maladies our ancestors could not face. The world has been converted to one location where everyone can experience through jet speed, communicate and commute to every nook and corner of the world. We are today better acquainted with the nature and styles of lives of all around the globe. We understand each other in the world in a much clearer way than before. We share the advantages of all the technical and scientific process developments, researches, innovations all across the world. We are even trying to explore accessing resources from other planets in the Universe.

What has been mentioned in the foregoing seems to be a little confusing on the developments as mentioned. The rub-off effect of the phenomenal advance in science & technology and their adoptions in the day today life, appear to be the over dependence on others for our essential and not so essential requirements, and consequent loss in self confidence and ability to manage globalised complexity. But the mute question remains as to how do we manage sanctity in our global business avenues? If the global craze and complexity leads to unethical behavior and conduct in managing our businesses, where do we pause and review, moderate and proceed? The major focus of the Directors and the In directors seems to be saddled between global opportunities and scandalous temptations for misdemeanor.

Case questions:

1) What are the pitfalls in the current scope of Corporate Governance (CG) Norms? What improvements and modifications do you suggest for effective implementation of CG?

2) Referring to the episodes in the above case study, which are the major reasons for the collapse of ethical standards of business conduct across the world in such cases? In the Indian economic and business climate as of to date

3) What are the major corrections or moderations do you recommend in the duties and accountability of Independent Directors? Should they have overriding authorities on the main promoters? (Directors, etc.)

11. Embracing and pursuing change

A.Case Study of an Insurance Company

Learning Objectives:

This case study focuses upon AEGON in the UK, part of the AEGON Group, one of the world's largest life insurance and pensions companies. AEGON owns pensions, life insurance, and asset management and adviser business in the UK. The case study illustrates the success that embracing and pursuing change has brought to AEGON in the UK.The Company was facing a strategic drift. To study the reason of low level of awareness impact on its ability to achieve its ambitions. To know about the imposing of prices by the government on goods which had led the reduction in profitability.It is helping AEGON move towards its goal of becoming the best long-term savings and protection business within the UK.

Synopsis:

With the changing expectations of customers, organisations constantly need to adapt to remain competitive. When faced with such pressures for change, managers may look for situations which are familiar to them. This may involve improving the ways in which they operate, but only little by little. This is called incremental change. The danger is that improving little by little might not be enough. They need to adapt to all of the bigger changes in the environment of that business as well. If they don't what happens is strategic drift.

Introduction:

The AEGON Group has 27000 employees and over 25 million

customers worldwide. Its major markets are in the USA and Netherlands. Since 1994, the UK has become another major and increasingly important market. In 1994 AEGON bought a large stake in Scottish Equitable was a strong brand with a heritage that went back to the 1830s. Since then AEGON's UK business has grown both organically and by acquiring other businesses.

As most of the acquired companies kept their existing identities, awareness of AEGON in the UK remained relatively low. AEGON realised that such low levels of awareness could impact on its ability to achieve its ambitions. Therefore, it needed to combine the global strength of its parent with the experience and reputation of the domestic company brands, like Scottish Equitable, that made up AEGON in the UK.

External factors influencing Change:

One of the main challenges for decision-makers is to understand the environment in which they are operating. They can then identify key issues which they need to respond to. Understanding these key issues improves decision-taking and reduces uncertainty. Few industries have experienced as many changes in their external environment in recent years as financial services.

Thinking ahead and saving for retirement is a concept that is sometimes difficult for people to understand. In the UK, life expectancy has risen in recent years so people can expect to be retired for longer. In many instances, individuals have not planned properly for retirement and there may be a shortfall in the amount of money available. There is also a drive by the government to reduce dependency on the State in old age. Added to this many companies have introduced new, less expensive pension schemes or insisted on employee pension contributions where they did not in the past. These factors mean people have to make decisions to invest properly at an earlier stage of their working lives. Investing in the future helps people to prepare in advance for old age. The benefits of such an investment are only realised years later.

The Industry:

The life insurance and pensions industry, in which AEGON operates, has had a poor reputation in recent years. Some organisations have been accused of 'Mis-selling' by not providing consumers with the best product for their needs. To prevent similar situations arising in the future the Financial Services Authority (FSA) has put significant amounts of regulation on the industry.

Financial services products are often difficult to understand. People do not always feel equipped to choose between the range of financial products and services and are not sure where to seek support and advice. In addition, falling values on the Stock Exchange have affected the investment return on some products, such as mortgage endowments. For some people this means that the product they bought has not delivered the financial return they expected. All this has created uncertainty in the financial services industry.

The industry has also been characterised by intense competition. AEGON is in competition with organisations which sell directly to consumers and which are better known in the UK. AEGON distributes its products and services to customers mainly through financial advisers. AEGON, as a reputable company, has had to address and overcome these industry-wide problems to remain competitive.

Reasons for change:

AEGON had historically been successful but government-imposed price controls had reduced profitability. Compared to its competitors, AEGON was not well known by consumers. It had developed good products and services and had a good reputation with distributors, particularly in the area of pensions which were a key strength of Scottish Equitable. However, it was not as well recognised in areas other than pensions. Often these other areas, such as offshore investment products, were more profitable. If consumers are to invest in a product long term, they need to know more about the organisation they are dealing with.

They need to recognise the brand and understand more about the brand values that it represents. As AEGON traded under a number of brand names it was not always easy for financial advisers and consumers to recognise the breadth and depth of the company in the UK.

How to move forward?

With a new Chief Executive (CEO) in place, AEGON underwent a discovery phase. The purpose of this was to find out what it had to do to meet the CEO's goal. This goal was to build 'the best long-term savings and protection business in the UK'. This time of discovery focused on three key questions:

1. What do we stand for in the UK?

2. What do we want to stand for in the UK?

3. What should we be doing about it?

Brand Audit:

To answer these questions AEGON undertook a brand audit. This audit looked at two aspects:

1. The company internally

2. How the organisation was positioned externally.

The purpose of the audit was to find out more information about the organisation. They helped AEGON to provide a more informed approach to the decisions that were needed to start the process of change. The audit showed that AEGON was solidly placed within the market. Its staff was known for their considerable expertise, innovation and clarity of communication. The external audit also helped to discover where AEGON was positioned in relation to its competitors. People were aware of AEGON saw it as being a refreshing and different organisation. However, there was evidence that people were confused about the breadth of what AEGON did because it traded under a number of different company brands.

Creating a New Culture is a Key part of Change Process :

Culture refers to the personality and attitude of an organisation. It also includes the shared beliefs, values and behavior of the employees. These determine the ways in which the organisation and its people make decisions and solve problems. The goal of AEGON's CEO helped to provide a vision for change. Financial objectives were important as the path for future developments depended upon these. It was also important to create more clarity about who AEGON was. With limited awareness of AEGON in the UK, it was important to explain what it had to offer, how big the organisation was within the UK and how strong it was globally. At the heart of this strategy was the need to:

1. Simplify financial services and provide more customer focus. It was important that consumers understood more precisely what they were buying, as well as the benefits and services they received

2. Develop the workforce. The objective was to develop the skills needed within the business to help it change. AEGON also created opportunities for progression from one job to

another in a way that provided individuals with a coherent career path.

3. Create a more distinct presence within the marketplace. This involved refreshing the AEGON brand in a way that made it more distinctive from its competitors and more attractive to customers.

A Behavioral Framework:

In order to help embed this culture, AEGON developed a behaviour framework to support its brand values. This was designed to influence how people at all levels within the organisation could work and make decisions. These behaviors emphasise the values of the organisation. They have helped to build AEGON's culture and have also influenced its performance. AEGON also introduced a Management Development Programme, supported by a leading Management College.

The eight behaviors are:

1. Think customer
2. Embrace change
3. Encourage excellence
4. Act with integrity
5. Decisive action
6. Work together
7. Learn and grow
8. Relate and communicate.

'Think customer' is about 'ensuring that the customer's needs are at the heart of our business, informing actions, decisions and behaviors'. For senior managers this means keeping the customer's experience at the heart of what AEGON does. Other managers and professionals are encouraged to 'innovate with your customers in mind'. All staff are encouraged to keep to commitments made to customers by doing 'what you say you will, when you say you will'.

Implementing the Change:

Before the change, consumers were confused about who AEGON was, what it did and how it fitted together. The audit had shown that global scale was important but so was local expertise. In the past, the AEGON brand had not been heavily promoted alongside Scottish Equitable or the other brand that it traded under. The brand strategy helped to reposition the brand within the industry. Now the association with AEGON is much stronger. For example, Scottish Equitable is now AEGON Scottish Equitable – reflecting both local knowledge and global power. All the brands are now carry a new common look which is refreshing and different. This, along with the values and behaviours, is helping to make the brand 'refreshingly different'.

Impacts of Change:

The changes affected the organization both internally and externally. Within the organization, they influenced not only how people behaved but also how they communicated. The organization has become more focused on the customer. The emphasis is on making information clearer for the customer to understand and the company easier to do business with. To help embed the values and behaviors, AEGON established a new relationship with Shirley Robertson, the famous yachtswoman and the only British female athlete to have won gold medal at consecutive Olympic Games. By associating Aegon with an individual who embodies similar values, it was able to bring the values and behaviors to life for staff.

However, AEGON had to develop the brand and its reputation. It did this in a number of ways:

1. External promotion campaigns emphasized the relationship between the Scottish Equitable and AEGON. This helped

to reinforce the local knowledge and the global power of AEGON in the UK.

2. The CEO talked to the media about the need of change. The refreshing of the brand internally and externally resulted in strong positive feedback.

3. AEGON has launched new and innovative products. For example, the 5 for Life annuity has helped to change the way in which consumers can look at their retirement income. It provides more certainty about levels of incomes for the consumer, with AEGON providing levels of return promised and being responsible for any risks associated with doing so.

Today the AEGON brand has a position from which it is influencing the financial services industry. It has posted record results with significant growth in underlying earnings. It has also increased its new business across a mix of profitable products and services, reflecting its continued strength.

Conclusions:

Change is continuous. The process of change is a journey. External factors will always be there to influence business organisation. AEGON responded to those factors by simplifying, clarifying and strengthening its brand in the UK. As organisations change, their patterns of behavior and business culture develop. For AEGON, this is a cycle in which the business uses its knowledge to learn from its experiences. This has helped AEGON as an organisation to move positively towards achieving its full potential and to remain competitive in an increasingly difficult market. (Business Case Studies LLP)

Case Questions:

1. What factors has led AEGON in Crises ?

2. State the strategy adopted by AGEON to comeback in market with full potential.

3. Do really the process of change has helped AEGON to occupy Market World?

12. The Big Brand Failures

Learning Objectives:

- Kingfisher Airlines Ltd. was owned by biggest liquor tycoon of India with an ambition to become an industry leader. Growing share in the aviation market, a wide number of destinations and numerous awards, depicted a very attractive and innovative picture for the company.

- Kingfisher airlines achieved success in gaining customer satisfaction by offering the great and comfortable flying experience to its passengers. However, with short impression. By the end of 2011, as a result of huge financial crisis; he was unable to repay loans to many public sector banks.

- The objective here is to describe the downfall of Kingfisher Airlines from the point of view of mistakes in strategic decision making.

Synopsis

About Kingfisher

In 2003, Kingfisher Airlines Limited was founded by Vijay Mallya as a premium and world-class airline group. The airline was based in Bangalore India and had more than 400 flights per day (Domestic & International). It used to be the most admired name in Asia-Pacific region.

Since 2005, as the airline-initiated operations, the business is proclaiming the losses. But after the company acquired Air Deccan in the year 2007, the situation became even more dreadful and this made the airline face financial issues for long.

Kingfisher Airlines holding second largest share in India's domestic air travel market till December 2011, faced extreme financial crisis.

The Rise, Dominance and Fall of Kingfisher **The Rise of Kingfisher Airlines**

On its peak time, it was the 2nd largest airline, in terms of carrying the number of passengers. The quality and comfortable service attracted many passengers in the initial years. And, then the Kingfisher acquired Air Deccan in 2007.

In just 3 years after touching the skies, the first international Bengaluru-London flight in 2008 was launched.

Marketing Strategy

They promoted the brand through all media channels like Radio, Television, Print, Multiplexes, Malls and in their In-flight magazines too.

- In just 2 years, the airlines achieved the aviation market share of 10%.

- During 2007, they had the most aggressive expansion plans of all Indian carriers.

- In June 2007, their influence in the market was increased with the acquisition of 26% shareholding of Air Deccan Airlines.

- During February 2009, more than 900,000 passengers flew with Kingfisher giving it the highest marketing share in India.

How Brand turned into Non-Performing Asset?

- By the end of the March 2008, company was under the debt

of INR 934 cr and net losses continued to widen in the following financial year.

- Acquisition of Air Deccan marked the end of Kingfisher Airlines. By the year 2009-10, airlines accumulated the debt of over INR 7,000 cr as the losses continued to pile up. 2010 was the year when it turned into a non-performing asset for banks.

- In 2012, the airlines operations were shut down as the DGCA suspended its flying license.

What Went Wrong?

- Lack of Delegation.

- Low-cost airline aviation airline, Air Deccan was treated as a step-child.

- Unnecessary Burning of Fuel.

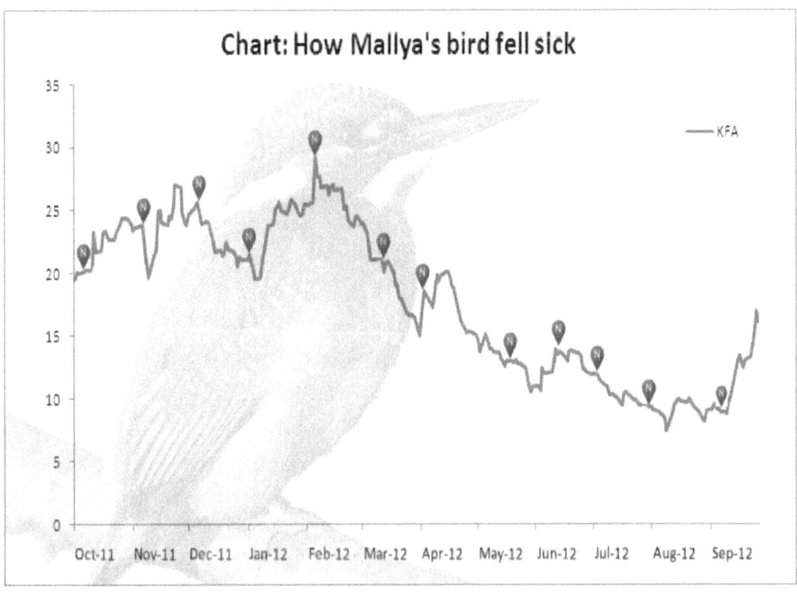

2. The Story of KODAK

The major reason that the brand was grounded was that it wasn't just into one business and trying hands on more than one business. The founder was taking care of different businesses personally without appointing proper CEOs and couldn't succeed in doing so. And, it's pretty obvious that if two brands serve almost the same service, then people would rather prefer the cheaper one.

Kodak failed in exploiting the constraints to elevate its performance and also lacked vision in developing new marketing strategies. Kodak failed to adapt the business design to changing conditions. They didn't forge or invested in Research and Development.

Due to lack of technological competence they suffered in balancing cost & technological support.

About Kodak

The American technology company, Kodak, was built on the culture of innovation and change in 1888. The company was invented and marketed by **George Eastmen** who was a former bank clerk from New York. At that time, it used to be a simple box camera, loaded with 100-exposure roll of film.

Kodak held a dominant position in photographic film in its time. Its tagline "Kodak Moments" was so famous that it was used for promoting events.

However, Kodak management's inability to see digital photography as a disruptive technology, even as its researchers extended the boundaries of the technology, would continue for decades.

Marketing Strategy of Kodak

The real genius of founder Eastman lied in his marketing

strategy. He launched an advertising campaign which featured children and women operating the camera with a slogan, **"You press the button, we do the rest."**

- In 1935, produced the first mass-market color film in 16 and 8mm.

- Kodak owned the film market with 90% market share in 1970s.

- Created the first digital camera in 1975.

Why Kodak Failed?

The first digital camera was designed by a Kodak engineer, Steve Sasson in 1975. It was a filmless photography at that time so they didn't want to threaten their film business so didn't do the marketing of the Digital camera. Whereas, other digital companies like Sony, Nikon, Fujifilm took the full advantage of the situation. Kodak missed the opportunities in the technology, they themselves invented.

- Kodak couldn't get on the nerve of the modern technology and remained in denial for long about digital photography while all the other brands adapted the change by introducing electronic cameras.

- Even before the digital photography they were failing to keep up as its rivalry Fujifilm started doing a better job than them.

- In January 2012, the big name went bankrupt because of not making the smart move into the digital world fast enough.

- On February 9, 2012, Kodak announced that it will exit the digital image capture business.

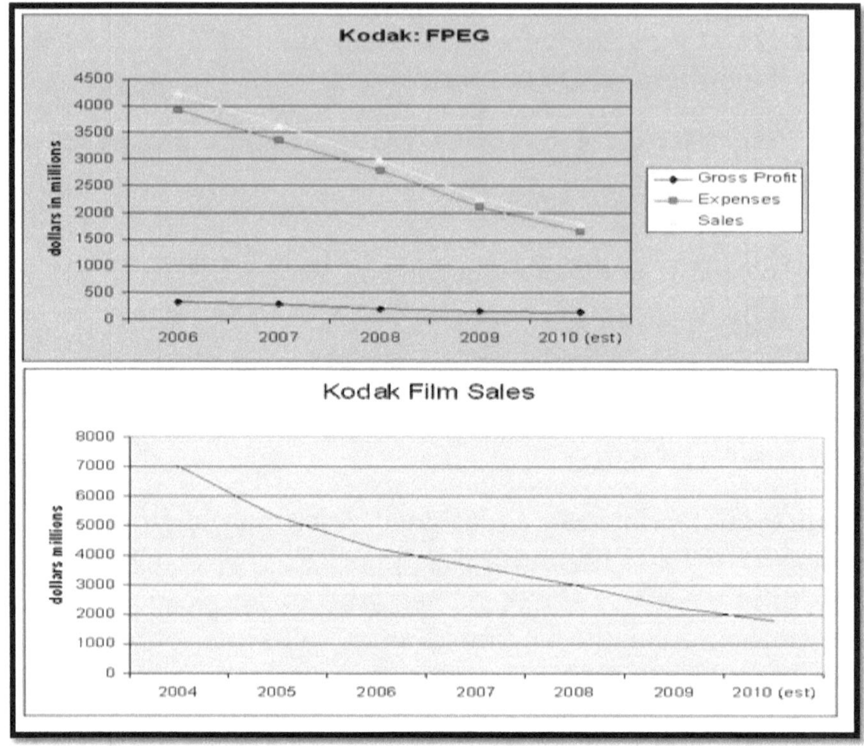

The much-expected journey of Kodak throughout its lifecycle What Went Wrong?

The Kodak failed due its slowness in transition. The world moved ahead with digital cameras, SD cards and USB cables but the company remained stuck with films. They didn't know how to respond in time and technology eventually killed the Kodak films.

How About Nokia?

Maintaining the brand value & strategy is a challenging journey, even when you reach great heights. Always take the right decision as single marketing blunder can destroy the brand completely.

In this age of rapidly changing technologies either the brand has to adapt the change with time or new trends. Those who refuse to improve becomes redundant and irrelevant to the industry one day.

The focus of the case study is to highlight marketing mistakes of Kodak which led ultimately to its downfall.

About Nokia

Nokia Corporation was founded in 1865 in Finland. The company was formally known as Nordic Mobile Telephone (NMT). The company name was changed to Nokia in 1871. They built the first international mobile phone in 1981 and this marked the beginning of the mobile era.

The Rise of Nokia, Connecting People

- Nokia phone was used in 1991 for making the first GSM call.

- In 1992, they launched Nokia 1101, the first GSM handset which became an instant hit.

- In 1988, Nokia became the world leader in mobile phones.

Marketing Strategy

- Nokia's Marketing share grew to 74% in March 2006 from 61.5%in October 2005.

- In the color phone category, market share jumped to 59.3% from 40.9%.

The Fall of Nokia

Nokia used to own a large portion of market of smartphone before the iPhone came out in market in 2007. Their refusal to change and learn new things lost their survival and this ultimately leaded to their demise. It used to be the leader in its market whereas Samsung was nowhere to be seen. But Samsung made the move at the right time and gained the success.

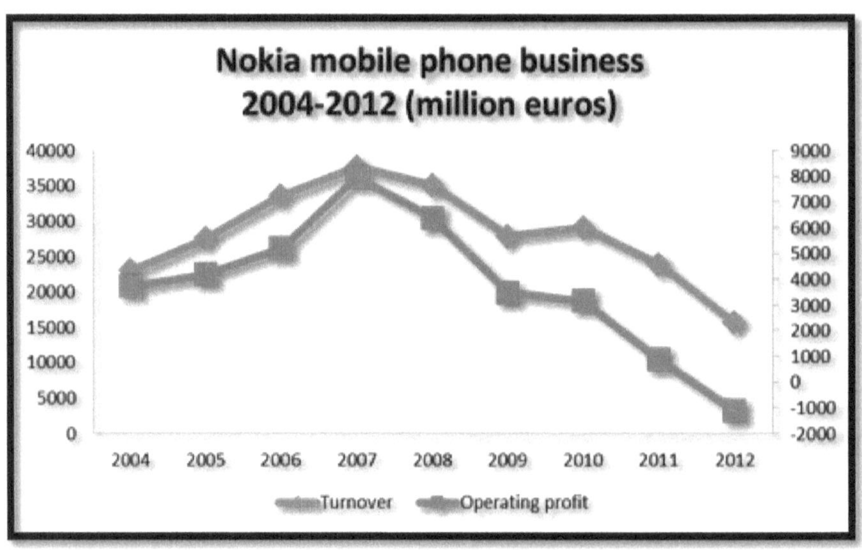

What Went Wrong?

The pioneer brand failed to respond to the completely changed smartphones with full touchscreen and application-based operating system. The years passed and they didn't keep up with the expectation of people and the consumers shifted. They remained their focus on the Symbian series. Until 2011, company didn't make the leap of faith onto the Windows phone and due to their slow response, they suffered such demise.

- **Nokia got acquired by Microsoft in 2013**

And as we conclude, we look forward to the statement made by Stephen Elop, Nokia's CEO in his speech when Nokia got acquired by Microsoft that "we didn't do anything wrong, but somehow, we lost". And, as far as the parameters on which success is measured, he was right somewhere that they didn't do anything wrong, it's just that they were unable to adapt the change at the right time and so, lost.

Conclusions:

The unwillingness to embrace the needed marketing change when required was probably the main cause that turned these brands down. One needs to think and act holistically for growing the brand with time otherwise, if you don't change, you will definitely get removed from the competition.

Nokia had been synonymous with all that was great in the early works of mobile phone technology. But they didn't keep up with technology i.e. smart phone which are inbuilt with advance features such as high pixel camera, web browsing, music on the go etc., and also, they failed to understand the current consumers requirements and the relationship people have with their phones as a communication partner, not just phones, Nokia had certainly understood they were about "Connecting with People". However, had their brand highlighted just been "Connecting", they would have continued to live a more relevant brand vision.

Creating a smaller company, owned by, but independent of, Eastman Kodak, would have been one step the company could have taken to better position themselves in the digital photography industry. Kodak does have a history of spinning off companies and buying smaller firms. In 1993, Eastman Chemical was turned into a separate corporation after being part of Eastman Kodak since 1920.

Because Kodak was the architect of their demise, in many people's eyes, the story becomes more interesting, but also more complicated. In the end, Kodak was not equipped to handle the technology they had initiated. This is not to say that the situation was out of their control or to excuse the decisions made, but once the digital photography market began to explode, Kodak was already too far behind to catch up.

Indian airline business has seen ideal growth and revolution which will go on in coming years. Many airlines come and go while the others have gained a strong ground in this business. The grand and ambitious Kingfisher Airline's project suffered huge downtime due to improper strategic decisions and mismanagement by the group. Instead of trying to utilize this grand airline project opportunity, Vijay Mallya focused to achieve a glamorous status. The airline became for the luxurious design, food and ambience including big goals for settling in international market but neglected the basic economic class. The strategy practiced by Vijay Mallya could not sustain for long and proved to be a great threat at a large scale to both, sustainability and stabilization of the aviation sector. Mallya is now the only board member left holding on to the brand. For a business to be successful the main focus should be on creating an efficient work-frame, taking appropriate decisions, establishing healthy competitive environment, improving quality of service and standing in unity to find best solutions to problems.

Case Questions

Q1). What was the relevance of strategic management to sustain competitive advantage of Nokia? Was Nokia capable enough to have Market-led approach?

Q2). What is your opinion on Change Management with regards to Kodak's perception of digital technology? Discuss the relevance of Kodak's Business Model to cope up with the competition and change.

Q3). What is your view on aggressive expansion strategy of Kingfisher? Do you think any change in marketing strategy at any stage would have increased the brand recovery chances for Kingfisher?

13. Ready for take-off?

A Case Study on Indian Ecommerce Industry

Learning Objectives

➤ To understand how the e-commerce industry deals with the requirement of logistics and warehouse.

➤ To understand how lack of communication is a huge challenge within the logistical chain.

➤ To study how effective the warehouse can account for customer preference to create the right label for business.

➤ To understand whether any changes in the economy can affect demand.

Synopsis

The industry has come a long way from the days, to become the backbone of the manufacturing and burgeoning e-commerce industry. The sector is evolving fast, with both the nature of the business and technology driving it, and undergoing dynamic changes. In the face of regulatory and infrastructural challenges, is the warehousing industry changing gears fast enough to support the growth that the Indian economy. Over a period of time warehousing industry in India has evolved from just brick and mortar shelters for the purpose of storing goods to highly sophisticated stockrooms, where, thanks to advanced tracking mechanism, each consignment can be tracked on a real time basis at the click of a button. Not just e-tail, in any industry segment, which deals with physical goods, warehouses play a vital role in the entire value chain from raw material to customer delight.

Specifically, in the manufacturing sector, with lean manu-facturing becoming the order of the day, a significant part of the functions from scheduling to labeling and packaging are being outsourced to third party logistics providers. But naturally the warehousing industry is gearing up, with the help of technology, to meet these new requirements. Let us understand the hardship and challenges faced by e-commerce industries.

Warehousing and logistics will be the key challenges for online firms joining the grocery retail party:

Global e-commerce giant Amazon recently piloted its grocery delivery process, branded Kirana Now, in Bengaluru wherein one could place orders via mobile phone. Home- bred Flipkart plans to go down the same path in the second half of this year. The market for food and grocery is set to get more competitive with players such as 24x7 Fresh, Pepper Tap, Falsabzi Just shop24 throwing their hats into the ring.

Though small and highly disintegrated at present, online grocery retailing in India is growing at 30 percent annually and is expected to touch Rs 270 crore by 2019 (according to a Ken Research report), thanks to the surge in the number of players operating in the industry. "This is the 'mother of all categories' in terms of size and the repetitive nature of the need. Grocery shopping is also the biggest pain point for the consumer," says K.Ganesh, a serial entrepreneur, and promoter in online grocery store Big Basket

Globally, grocery retailing - which comprise 60-70 percent of traditional brick-and-mortar-retailing - seems to be the next frontier for online firms to conquer because that segment is still relatively untapped. A new study, "e-commerce Supply Chain Insights in Groceries and Consumer Packaged Goods in the United States (February 2015)", by Amitabh Sinha of University of Michigan and Paul Wetzel of Willard Bishop (with research assistance by Manqi Li, Jianyu Liu), shows that even in the

US, e-commerce in the grocery and consumer packaged goods (CPG) sector is lagging. It currently only accounts for about 3 percent of total sales. But the authors expect the sector to grow rapidly across all e-commerce retailers, including pure-play and brick and mortar stores. "Brick and mortar retailers that also have e-commerce operations are moving toward an Omni-channel strategy," the report says.

While the potential is obvious, selling groceries online is a bigger challenge than any other category, given the complexities of supply chain management, logistics, relatively low margins, and the consumer need for quick fulfillment. "This is not a game for angel investors and early-stage VCs-margins are low and scale is important. Since 2012 there were 40 companies of which only three have managed to raise money and 30 of them have shut shop," adds Ganesh.

Eye on stock management

Managing inventory is the most challenging task for any player in this space, especially if it follows an inventory-led business model. Delivering on the promise of reaching perishable items in the mint-fresh condition is easier said than done. Big Basket has tied up with around 400 suppliers such as large FMCG companies like P&G, Unilever, Kellogg, institutional farmers, importers, and aggregators to source products that they wish to sell to the final consumer. Hence, it is critical to hold small inventory as more inventory means more storage space and probably more wastage. On the other hand, too little inventory may mean falling short of consumer expectations.

But how do you determine the ideal inventory amount? This will require forecasting and a well-oiled turnaround mechanism. Technology is the biggest facilitator in this. "If you plan and rotate the inventory with the help of technology, you can ensure minimum capital compared to a brick and mortar stores where the minimum holding period for inventory is between 25 and 30 days," says Rajiv Tetviya, co-founder, **Green cart**. Green cart stocks gourmet and grocery products based on daily and monthly requirements.

Big Basket also manages its orders with the help of algorithms that factor in sales rates, seasonality of products, suppliers' frequency of delivery, their performance in the past, and so on. Even order placements are forecasted with the help of algorithms, which can be adjusted to factor in variables such as promotional offers or a new launch, both of which can trigger changes in consumer demand patterns. Co-founder Vipul Parekh says the firm operates with 10-day inventory, with perishable items like fruits and vegetables having a smaller window of a day and a half.

Big Basket operates in Bangalore, Mumbai, Hyderabad, Pune, and Chennai and has a warehouse in each of these cities. The suppliers deliver at the centralized distribution center where inventory is held and delivered to the transshipment points or customer's premises directly. The company has invested around Rs 30-40 crore per warehouse and around 20 percent of its investment is towards technology.

Now consider **ZopNow**, an online grocery store based in Bangalore, which has gone through a shift in its business model. The company used to manage its inventory in the past but switched to a tie-up with offline retailer Hyper City. "We save on rentals of warehouse and other associated capital costs," says Mukesh Singh, CEO, ZopNow. Since it delivers from stores located in the central part of a city, its shipment costs have gone down dramatically. Almost 40 percent of its orders are now delivered in less than 90 minutes from the time it takes the order; in some cases, the delivery time is as low as 30 minutes. "It opens up the entire Omni-channel route for us where offline and online businesses can work together to pass on the benefit to the consumer," adds Singh. The company plans to step into Pune, Mumbai, and Hyderabad in some time.

On its part, Local Banya employs a mix of just in time (JIT) sourcing and warehousing. Fast-moving items such as staples are stocked in warehouses as there is a steady and measurable demand for them. For other items, it uses JIT, procuring things from vendors and suppliers on an as-per-need basis. "It is not possible to warehouse everything. So we have to employ this mix efficiently," says Karan Mehrotra, co-founder, Local Banya.

Keeping it fresh

It is important to ensure perishable items reach the customer without delay or damage. As soon as an item of food is delivered to Big basket's warehouse, it goes for a quality check, cleaning of debris and mud, segregation of dead leaves, etc., followed by packaging and labeling before finally hitting the shelves. More than 80 percent of its orders are for fresh produce. "You need to innovate and think of solutions that would work in the Indian market. That means looking for local suppliers for equipment, products, and so on," adds Parekh. Another new entrant, **Falsabzi**, has earmarked an investment of Rs 100 crore in the next five years. "Our operating margin will be 30 percent and rest we want to pass on to the consumer," says Rajesh Gupta, chairman, RSND Group.

Some players have started branding products that they sell. "Any company in this space has to build its brand of staples and other items but it will require deep sourcing expertise on where and how to source the best products at a competitive price and consistent quality," adds Ganesh.

Meanwhile, Pepper Tap, an on-demand hyper local grocery delivery company, claims that 90 percent of its transactions come through the mobile. Pepper Tap connects directly with the local vendors and supermarkets and promises delivery in two hours. It is working on a marketplace model. "We didn't want to incur a lot of capital cost involved in setting up or manning a warehouse," says Navneet Singh, co-founder, Pepper Tap.

But that has its challenges. "A major constraint in the store pick models is reduced margins since the company will have to share it with stores they operate with," adds Parekh. To get around this, Big Basket is tying up with local kirana stores in Bangalore to supply the inventory to local stores. In this model, the company has more control over the supply quality and the availability of products.

People movement & logistics

Technology can also help in picking, packing, and delivering orders accurately. In the cold chain facility at Green cart's warehouse, employees follow a specific code of conduct to ensure there is a minimum human touch involved in the entire process of handling fresh produce. So far the company has invested more than Rs 50 lakh in its cold chain. "Human processes and their integration with technology have improved productivity for Green cart by almost three times," claims Tetviya. The company works on the "relay race principle" where it takes less than three minutes to process an order.

At Big basket, the warehouse is designed in a manner that minimizes the path a picker has to cover, thus saving on time. It has around 400 vans to manage its operations.

Green cart has drawn up a service level agreement with set standards that all its suppliers have to adhere to. The onus for a product past its expiry date lies with the supplier. Big Basket is working with a few recycling companies to dispose of organic waste. Technology plays a crucial role in the last-mile as well. It is now working to introduce a 'track your exact time of delivery' feature. Most of the ZopNowvans are also GPS tagged and orders are geo-fenced to give an insight into the time it takes to deliver, helping it to map the delivery processes accurately.

"The average delivery time was about 95 to 100 minutes and with technology, in some places, we have been able to reduce it to 60 minutes," says Singh of Pepper Tap.

Outcomes

India growth in online grocery retailing due to Global e – commerce in spite of facing inventory and warehousing challenges is remarkable. Though the requirement of forecasting and a well-oiled turnaround mechanism is needed and technology is the biggest facilitator in this. Various organizations are coming up with various models to make smooth flow of inventory and in all this process technology is providing an add on advantage to all the organizations with all trending features to ensure delivery of product takes place on time and with accuracy

Conclusions:

E-commerce industry is definitely a boon to Indian economy but at the same time certain challenges and obstacles with respect to logistics and warehousing are not allowing the industry to go ahead and take country's economy to the next level. So it is important that these obstacles and challenges should be tackled and the customers should be given a hassle free service which will really have a positive overall impact on the business of these industries.

Case Questions :

1. As per the growing business of the E-commerce industry

do you think that warehousing and logistics have become a challenge and if yes, can you suggest strategies to overcome the same?

2. How should perishable products treated by such companies to ensure that customers get such products on time and without damaging its perishable nature of the product?

3. Can the role of technology in this sector be a boon?

14. Biyani VS Ambani

A Case study on The E- commerce Tussle

Learning Objectives:-

1. To evaluate various opportunities on an ongoing basis.

2. Trying to figure out the Indian consumer and crack the retail code.

3. The industrial mindset to focus on logistics, distribution and supply chain helped.

Synopsis:

In any new sector, be it airline, telecom or retail, one pioneer gives it a start and it is up to the second business to take it to the next level. The belief is that, as in most global markets, a homegrown retailer will set the marker in India and Reliance wants to be that homegrown retailer. RIL is not looking at taking a pie of the existing market and is focused on growing the market.

Case details:

It's no comparison, Kishore Biyani says calmly down a phone line, about a storyline that seeks to compare his business, personality and operating style with that of an industry captain who might be his nearest competitor in the retail business, but whose main business generates more in profits than Biyani's does in revenues.

Out of reverence for MukeshAmbani and rare reticence on his own part, Biyani declines to speak for this story. But the storyline

—Biyani versus Ambani; Future Group versus Reliance Retail — won't go away. If anything, it has acquired an immediacy that is all the more compelling for the contrasts it throws up.

There are Reliance Retail's latest financial results. Announced last week as part of the results of its parent, Reliance Industries Limited (RIL), those numbers show that, in terms of annual turnover, Reliance Retail has crossed Rs 10,000 crore and is breathing down Future Group's neck, which had a nine-year head start. From Rs 4,271 crore in 2010, the gap in revenues has closed to, analysts estimate, about Rs 2,000 crore.

Another year and Reliance might inch ahead. There are people movements. A handful of trusty, senior Biyani aides have changed sides, notably Sanjay Jog and Damodar Mall, and this has caused some consternation to a man who is known to wear his heart on his sleeve even when running a Rs 12,000-crore retail empire. "We always have an emotional relationship with our employees. So, it can be difficult during parting," Biyani had told ET last month during an interaction for another story.

And there are the contrasts. Both businesses stand at pivotal — and strikingly contrasting — points in their respective journeys. While Future resembles a bird whose wings have been clipped, Reliance is taking flight. While Future is in rebuilding mode, Reliance is taking its building to another level. While Biyani is returning from a "vanvas" (exile) to play a larger role in Future, Ambani, who too declined to speak for this story, is a distant presence in Reliance's operating frame, which is dominated by Manoj Modi, his right-hand man, and is populated with experienced Indian and expat retail professionals.

Rebuilding Vs Building

For the moment, the spotlight is on Reliance. Ever since Ambani marked out retail as the next business focus area for RIL in 2006, he has been talking about a breakout at almost every shareholder meeting of his flagship. Last year might have been just that. Arvind Singhal, chairman of Technopak Advisors, a retail consultant firm, asks to draw pause and think back. "Future Group has been in retail for 18 years, Shoppers Stop for 15 years, the Tata group also started 15 years back," he says. "So, I think, it is remarkable that Reliance has been able to overtake some of them in five to six years." And now, it has Future in its sights. Being a late entrant into the retail business has helped Reliance, feels Abneesh Roy, vice-president of Edelweiss Securities, a financial services and research firm.

"In any new sector, be it airline, telecom or retail, one pioneer gives it a start and it is up to the second player to take it to the next level," he says, pointing out how early pioneers like Shoppers Stop in lifestyle and food retailers in the South are now also-rans. "Reliance has learnt from the failures of its peers. So, it was able to work out the right permutations and is now in a sweet spot."

Inside Reliance Retail, the belief is that, as in most global markets, a homegrown retailer will set the marker in India. And Reliance wants to be that homegrown retailer. "It is like China, where although Walmart and Carrefour have been present for 15-20 years, they are still given a run for their monies by traditional players," says a senior Reliance Retail official, on the condition of anonymity.

Because it has a more significant presence in specialty segments (for example, jewelry or electronics), Reliance is competing not just with the Future Group, but also beyond. "The market is getting segmented," says Kumar Rajgopalan, president of the Retail Association of India. "The challenge for Reliance, which is in several formats, including specialty stores such as Reliance Jewels, will be to fight the biggies in such different verticals.

For instance, Tata's 'Tanishq' is a big competitor in the jewelry space." Similarly, in the consumer electronics space, it is pitted against Tata Croma and Vijay Sales, among others. "Retailers in consumer electronics have been competing to differentiate themselves with limited success," says the Reliance official. "We have chosen to do things differently. We are betting big on the services played here, in pre- and after- sales so that it creates a different brand perception and pulls consumers." Given where the Indian market is now, the position in the pecking order — one or two — is somewhat academic, feels Thomas Varghese, former president of the retail council of the Confederation of Indian industry and current chairman of the CIS National Council of Marketing. "The organised retail market is still nascent and there is enough room for everyone to grow."

"We are not looking at taking a pie of the existing market and are focused on growing the market," says the Reliance official. Several Future Group officials, who spoke off the record for this story, expressed a similar line of thought.

The Future Group, anyway, has plenty to think about besides growth. Years of unfettered growth, fuelled by debt, caught up with it. "Earlier, there was nothing to lose. So, there was less fear during the stage of creation. Today, there is another fear, of losing what we created," he told ET last month. Most of 2012 was about course correction. It saw Biyani sell some businesses completely (financial services and insurance) and give up significant ownership in others (Pantaloons). And it saw Biyani return from driving from the back seat to taking the steering wheel again.

Intuition Vs Precision

Biyani is back roaming the stores, trying to figure out the Indian consumer and crack the retail code. In the way he built Future Group, Biyani relied immensely on intuition and on-the ground observations. A senior Future Group official, who did not want to be named, narrates one such incident. "We were standing in front of one of our stores. KB (as everyone calls him) predicted what the sales would be at the end of the day within an hour of observing consumers coming out with various sizes of bags," he says. "He did not need a calculated system projecting target sales."

Ambani does walk the Reliance aisles, and even passes on feedback down the rank and file. But his frequency and intensity is nothing compared to that of Biyani, who goes into the granular during his regular store visits and is not even averse to making it company policy. "He would observe consumers from different income strata or communities and comment on how a particular community had begun shopping at their stores or how a particular community was conspicuous by their absence." If the focus of the Future Group has been the front end, Reliance's has been the back end, the less visible and the less glamorous part of the retail business.

"The effort begins before the match," says the Reliance official. Reliance approached the supply chain and processes with its trademark engineering mindset and with help from retail professionals who cut their teeth in the world's biggest and best retailers. Its two big hires came in 2011: Rob Cissell, former chief operating officer of Walmart China, was drafted in as CEO of Reliance Value Retail; and Shawn Gray, who headed store operations in the Chinese company, came in as COO. "The supply chain cannot be outsourced, it is the heart of the business," Cissell told ET in August 2012.

Singhal of Technopak says this sharp focus on the back end has been critical to Reliance's relative success. "Reliance built a strong foundation for the business not just in terms of IT, but also in terms of hiring the right kind of talent and consultants from all across the world with the right knowledge," he says.

"So, they did not have to make all the mistakes themselves. That **industrial mindset to focus on logistics, distribution and supply chain helped."**

The Reliance official cites Reliance Trends, its fashion format, as an example of an efficient back end creating value at the front end. "The entire business was engineered in a way that sourcing capability, designers, supply chain and distribution were in the right sync to ensure that affordable, yet fashionable, products reached the consumer in the right fashion cycle," he says. Acknowledging the strides Reliance has taken in many facets of the retail business, Singhal feels the company is still weak on the soft skills needed in a consumer-facing business. "To proactively anticipate customer needs, which is partly science, intuition and emotions," he says. "India has been an under-served market. So, consumers have been very generous with system flaws initially. But they are getting more aspirational and Reliance will have to shift gears and lay more emphasis on consumer-facing attributes."

Family Vs Professionals

The wheels of change in Reliance are being driven by a battery of professionals, including about 10 expats and several old Future group hands. «It used expats and experts with different skills from various global retail entities with a consistency that Future Group did not,» says Roy. «One is very entrepreneur-led and the other has a very corporate approach,» adds Varghese. About two years back, Biyani had moved out of day-to-day operations in the Future Group, and the organization was seen as having lost some of its energy. He's back now, and stamping his presence. "I am bringing in fresh energy into the business. Employees look towards their leader for inspiration and I realise that I have to do that," he told ET last month.

Reliance Retail, by comparison, is led by Manoj Modi, Mukesh's loyal lieutenant. For all of Reliance being a promoter-led operation and Modi's influence, Reliance Retail is seen as a collective where a vision has been communicated and the second and third rungs are empowered. «In Reliance Retail, there are no tall people," says the Reliance official. "We are like an army." This official adds that select individuals cannot make a difference in the retail business. "Our culture is built with   a focus on the supply chain and is very process-oriented," he says. "We are paranoid about processes. It is a religion for us. So, at times, it may seem bureaucratic."

While the contrasts will shape their choices and outcomes, both outfits can stand tall in their respective territories without bothering about competing with each other, feels Kavil Ramachandran, professor at the Indian School of Business. "At the end of the day, RoI (return on investment) is more important than mere generation of turnover," he says. "And as an entrepreneur, probably, Biyani has more flexibility to move faster than a large corporate like Reliance. Having said that, nothing would stop Reliance in its growth path given its background of setting an ambitious vision and backing it with adequate resources and a 'do it' culture."

Conclusions:

It is necessary to merge with companies to attract the investors and growth of the company. Merging helps to create a good vision and mission for the company. Companies are usually in their initial phase of growth and their stocks have the potential for substantial appreciation in price. There are several key factors that must be considered when evaluating investment of growth.

Case questions:

1. How would you analyse the two distinct business management Strategies applied by the Biyanis of the Future Group & The giants Ambanis. Which one do you think will be a winner in the long run??

2. With the relaxed FDI norms (In Spite of certain regulatory

hurdles) and influx of Global Retail Giants in the Indian Retail Scenario. There obviously is likely to be a tough fight between Entrepreneurial approach(Followed by Many Existing Indian Retail Cos) and highly professionalized and time tested Global giants warring for space in the highly promising organized retail segment in India. How would you rate the prospects for the existing players in the long term.??

3. What is important in the likely future scenario- focus on Front End Retail or effective management of the Logistics of retail(Back End) in terms of Product quality & Customer Focus??

15. Chasing the long tail

A Case Study on E-Commerce

Learning Objectives:

1. To evaluate the Long Tail Marketing strategy & its applications.

2. To analyze the effects of online retailing at the advent of Covid 19, the challenges & threats that the fixed retailers face.

3. To analyze the change in e-commerce due to the increase in online retailing.

4. To analyze the supply & demand on various products, their availability, Customer satisfaction & sales.

Synopsis

E-Commerce involves the transaction of goods and services, the transfer of funds and the exchange of data. It draws on technologies like mobile commerce, electronic funds transfer, supply chain management, Internet marketing, & online transaction processing. In recent days, on sudden, unexpected advent of Covid 19, e-commerce has reached a higher place in the world of digitalization. This case study highlights online shopping verses traditional marketing. It also highlights the products which were of less importance & less in demand by consumers until the Covid 19 pandemic situation, gained more demand by young entrepreneurs to showcase their products on online retailing market places.

The spread of online retailing has spawned many internet

entrepreneurs hawking obscure or regionally known products. So when is the long tail market viable?

India's e-commerce story is no longer limited to billion-dollar valuations and discount-crazy consumers thronging shopping websites. The online marketplace has now become an incubator for entrepreneurs who are hawking rare, obscure or even unpopular products. The shift was inevitable. The search for differentiation in an environment of cut-throat price competition has taken marketplaces like Snap deal, Myntra, Pepper fry and Fashionara to the doorstep of many small, regional brands and makers of niche products, who are now able to sell their products across the country without worrying about managing logistics or marketing. Says Sandeep Komaravelly, Senior Vice-President, Marketing, Snapdeal, *"The online platform enables this transaction between sellers and buyers at zero upfront cost, and hence, the size of the business is not a pre-condition. This is how the online marketplace model democratizes entrepreneurism andbusiness growth by giving people more options."*

So while analysts continue to question the sustainability of   a model driven by heavy discounting, some   marketplaces are already chasing the long tail, tapping demand that is unarticulated and translating it into incremental sales. And since the internet makes distribution easier and uses state-of-the-art recommendation techniques to help consumers become aware of more obscure products, niches that weren't popular are now being discovered by consumers.

The simple truth is, the long tail makes little economic sense in a physical world because stores only have so much shelf space and any brand/product stocked needs to justify its presence on the shelves by selling a requisite amount. On the other hand, it costs a Snap deal nothing to put a rare, not-really-top-of-mind product on its catalogue, and sell a couple every week. Sure, it may never become a smash hit, but some sales in the long tail do add up to a significant market size.

In that sense, e-commerce has the potential to queer the pitch for the short head - large-volume, mass market products. Says SudhirVoleti, Assistant Professor, Marketing, **ISB**, "The long-tail model is about finding demand that is latent and players who find this latent demand will succeed."

Product is the Hero

At the end of the day, says Ganesh Subramanian, COO, **Myntra**, the hero of this story is the product, which is offered at a good price. He believes, online platforms are a great opportunity for sellers since young buyers are willing to experiment. *"In terms of value, a third of our business comes from small-and medium-sized brands. We help with marketing support but success hinges on the product,"* he says adding that while building scale to keep pace with growing demand can be tricky for a small producer, it is not impossible - one of his regional partners, for instance, has scaled Rs.50 Crores in revenue in two years.

Indeed, there are many such stories of internet entrepreneurs who ditched their jobs to sell fun products online. Some started for a lark, but now have credible businesses and are now building scale. Rahul Khullar, CEO & founder, **Style HomezInc**, for instance, decided to sell bean bags from his home in 2013 in Delhi. His relationship with Snapdeal began in November 2013. From 30-40 pieces a month, Khullar now sells 3,200 pieces. Says Khullar, *"We grew 100 times in one year and the branding support that Snap deal provided through newspaper inserts and via Google ads drew customers to our website and urged them to check out our products."* The brand today services more pin codes in the country than it had hoped for in 2013. The team has also grown and stands at 35 people right now.

Anupam Barman, a silk sari retailer based in Varanasi, has seen his sales jump 25 per cent in 2014 compared to the previous year, after Snap deal approached him to sell his products on the portal. Not only has Barman found a new audience for his woven silks, he now gets to connect with the consumers directly and gets feedback on what products sell well and which ones require a bigger push.

Khullar of Style Homez says that since his venture was self-funded, it did not have the required financial muscle to invest in brand building. But its relationship with Snap deal gave it instant visibility. What has worked to his advantage is the payments cycle, which coincides with a sale.

Kitsch is the King

One visible trend is that most marketplaces are reaching out to people who either manufacture or deal in kitschy products. Arun Sirdeshmukh, founder of **Fashionara**, says unusual products that are not found in physical stores do well on online channels. Unusual gift items or trinkets are known to attract millennials who tend to shop more frequently online.

Given that most of these merchants are not really bred-in- the-bone merchants they need support in product selection and in showcasing them online. Most marketplaces help merchants build their e-catalogue and in listing them on the platform. In many cases even the product descriptions and photo shoots are facilitated by the e-commerce platform.

Even when it comes to inventory management, the shopping portals give inputs to the sellers on the minimum inventory they need to hold at any given point in time according to the category. AkshayJuneja, founder of **Fabdeal**, an ethnic wear brand from Surat that sells on Myntra, says that Myntra gives his team a heads-up on how their stock is doing and how many pieces of which design they should they hold. Says Juneja,*"The advantage of this relationship is global reach. When we were offline we could only sell to local customers; now we reach overseas audience as well. From 50 pieces a day, our sales have gone* *up to 200-300 pieces a day. During the festive season, Fabdeal had to organize delivery of 600 pieces a day."*

That said, some analysts are wary of the long tail theory's implicit challenge to the Pareto principle - or the so-called 80-20 rule, which would make it appear that there was a greater importance of the hit products - and warn the long tail theory may not be universally applicable. In a working paper titled, *"Is Tom Cruise Threatened? Using Netflix Prize Data to Examine the Long Tail of Electronic Commerce,"* Wharton Operations and Information Management professor SergueiNetessine and doctoral student, Tom F Tan contended that while the long tail effect holds true in some cases, mass appeal products retain their importance when expanding product variety and consumer demand are factoring in.

"There are companies based on the premise of the Long Tail effect that argue they will make money focusing on niche markets," says Netessine. *"Our findings show it is very rare in business that everything is so black and white. In most situations, the answer is, 'It depends.' The presence of the Long Tail effect might be less universal than one may be led to believe."*

According to Netessine, "The Long Tail effect may be present in some cases, but few companies operate in a pure digital distribution system. Instead, they must weigh supply chain costs of physical products against the potential gain of capturing single customers of obscure offerings. Companies must also consider the time it takes for consumers to locate off-beat items they may want." *(Source: Rethinking the Long Tail Theory: How to Define 'Hits' and 'Niches', Knowledge@Wharton)* Also the task before the curated marketplaces is far from easy. They have to evaluate the products for their quality and the vendor for his reliability to be able to make a difference in the market. Most of the marketplaces have separate quality teams to monitor products, quality and catalogue. Mind you, this is not a one-time effort but has to be done continuously. That apart, the onus of distribution also lies with the marketplace. On receiving an order a marketplace will connect with the relevant vendor and take care of the packaging and delivery within the promised time. Managing reverse logistics - ferrying returned products – is also handled by the concerned marketplace.

Handholding new entrepreneurs might be a wonderful thing and the long tail might earn e-commerce players rich dividends, but is the model sustainable? Most sellers on these market places are growing at breakneck speed and if this growth continues, they will have to scale up rapidly to meet demand. Failure to meet demand or quality expectations would not only harm the vendor, it has the potential to hurt the credibility of the marketplace as well. Fashionara's Sirdeshmukh, however, does not believe it is an issue. Most marketplaces use advanced predictive analytics to get a sense of future demand. If they sense that a vendor cannot meet the demand, the easiest thing to do is to remove the vendor's catalogue from the site. Subramanian of Myntra says, *"The growth of these smaller brands will be determined by their ability to scale up. They have to invest in infrastructure."*

Most e-commerce portals believe that this trend will play out in two ways. Some of these brands will emerge as strong standalone brands in their own right. If and when they do, they would want to migrate to their own websites. On the other hand, some will remain niche and only cater to an audience their inventory allows them to service. However, maintaining quality and managing the time-to-consumer-doorstep will continue to be the biggest challenges on their way.

Conclusions

E-commerce provides multiple benefits to the consumers in form of availability of goods at lower cost, wider choice and saves time. Many young entrepreneurs have opted for online retailing reaching the vendors of unpopular products. Online retail market place has now become the most sought destination by the entrepreneurs for constant profitable products. The products which were less known & less in demand as well, until the Covid pandemic situation.

Case questions :

1. Explain how can Long Tail theory of marketing be achieved in post corona pandemic situation? Give examples.

2. What are the factors that influence the steady revenue from less demand products and at the same time catering to the need of the consumers?

3. Explain the applications of Long Tail Theory of Marketing strategy in online retailing.

16. Domino's India Supply Chain Management

A Case study on Supply Chain Management

Learning Objectives :

The main learning objective of this case study is to study the components of the supply chain of a fast food company and its effective management with special reference to Dominos pizza. This case also focus on competitive analysis in pizza sector specially the competition between Domino's and McDonalds. To study the different logistics models for improving the overall business is also one of the objectives of the case.

Synopsis

In the view of business expansion Domino's revamped its supply chain operations in India. Initially Domino's have the simple logistics model. The case discusses the various benefits of the new logistics model and discusses the reasons for the revamp. The benefit of low costs achieved through the new model was passed on to the customers in the form of lower prices. The case also compares Domino's new supply chain model with McDonald's supply chain model.

Introduction

In early 2000, Pawan Bhatia (Bhatia), the CEO of Domino's Pizza India (Domino's) was a man in a hurry. Ever since Bhatia took over as the CEO of Domino's in November 1999, he had been frantically reworking the pizza chain's India strategy. Bhatia was planning to open 150 new outlets by the end of 2002 covering 23 cities including Bhubaneshwar (Orissa) and Jamshedpur (Bihar). In late 1999, Indocean Chase, the private equity fund bought a 25% stake in Domino's operations in India from the Delhi-based industrial family, the Bhartias, who held Domino's franchise in India. Domino's told investment bankers at the fund that it planned to go in for an initial public offering (IPO) in the next two years. Indocean Chase advised Domino's to go beyond its 16 outlets in Delhi to exploit the potential in the pizza delivery business. Unless a well-thought-out expansion plan was put into place, the IPO was unlikely to find too many takers.

As part of its expansion plans Domino's revamped its entire supply chain operations, from sourcing raw materials to shipping them for processing at a central location to delivering it to the customer's. Initially, Domino's had a simple model. It had three self-contained commissaries in New Delhi, Mumbai and Bangalore which bought their own wheat, tomatoes and other ingredients, processed them, then delivered them in refrigerated trucks to each outlet. However, volumes were expected to increase when Domino's planned to open new outlets. Therefore, the existing model had to be revamped. Bhatia said, "It's crucial for us to build a low-cost supply chain operation which takes costs out of the system and in turn gives us greater pricing flexibility in the marketplace."Analysts felt that Domino's had to rethink its supply chain operation because it was the biggest area of costs. Since 75% of Domino's customers ordered either from office or home, it did not have to lease large plots of land in prime locations to attract traffic. Instead, it needed an efficiently managed call center to bring better returns. In the late 1950s, Dominick De Varti (Varti) owned a small pizza store named Domi Nick's Pizza on the Eastern Michigan University campus in Ypsilanti, Michigan. In 1960, two brothers who were students of the University of Michigan - Thomas S. Monaghan (Thomas) and James S.Monaghan (James) - bought the store for US$900. In 1961, James sold his share of business to Thomas.

The pizza business did well and by 1965, Thomas was able   to open two more stores in the town-Pizza King and Pizza from the Prop. Within a year, Varti opened a pizza store in a neighborhood town with the same name, Domi Nick's Pizza. Thomas decided to change the name of his first store, Domi Nick's Pizza, and one of his employees suggested the name Domino's Pizza(Domino's). The advantage of this name Thomas felt was that it would be listed after Domi Nick in the directory. Domino's philosophy rested on two principles - limited menu and delivering hot and fresh pizzas within half-an-hour. In 1967, it opened the first franchise store in Ypsilanti, and in 1968, a franchise store in Burlington, Vermont.

However, the company ran into problems when its headquarters (the first store) and commissary were destroyed by fire. In the early 1970s, the company faced problems again when it was sued by Amstar, the parent company of Domino Sugar for trademark infringement. Thomas started looking for a new name and came up with Red Domino's and Pizza's Dispatch. However, there wasn't any need for it because Domino's won the lawsuit in 1980.In 1982, Domino's Pizza established Domino's Pizza International (DPI) that was made responsible for opening Domino's stores internationally. The first store was opened in Winnipeg, Canada. Within a year, DPI spread to more than 50 countries and in 1983, it inaugurated its1000th store (Refer Exhibit II for worldwide revenues).

Around the same time, new pizza chains like Pizza Hut and Little Caesar established themselves in the US. Domino's Pizza faced intense competition because it had not changed its menu of traditional hand-tossed pizza. The other pizza chains offered low-priced breadsticks, salads and other fast food apart from pizzas. Domino's faced tough competition from Pizza Hut in the home delivery segment also. Little Caesar was eating into Domino's market share with its innovative marketing strategies. By 1989, Domino's sales had reduced significantly and cash flows were affected due to the acquisition of assets. In

1993, Thomas took measures to expand Domino's product line, in an attempt to revive the company and tackle competition.

The company introduced pan pizza and bread sticks in the US. In late 1993, Domino's introduced the Ultimate Deep Dish Pizza and Crunchy Thin Crust Pizza. In 1994, it rolled out another non-pizza dish - Buffalo Wings. Though Domino's did not experiment with its menu for many years, the company adopted innovative ways in managing a pizza store.

Thomas gave about 90% of the franchisee agreements in the US to people who had worked as drivers with Domino's. The company gave ownership to qualified people, after they had successfully managed a pizza store for a year and had completed a training course. Domino's also gave franchises to candidates recommended by existing franchisees. Outside the US, most of Domino's stores were franchise-owned. Domino's was also credited for many innovations in the pizza industry and setting standards for other pizza companies. It had developed dough trays, corrugated pizza boxes, insulated bags for delivering pizzas, and conveyor ovens.

In 1993, Domino's withdrew the guarantee of delivering pizzas within 30-minutes of order and started emphasizing on Total Satisfaction Guarantee (TSG) which read: "If for any reason, you are dissatisfied with your Domino's Pizza dining experience, we will re-make your pizza or refund your money." Domino's entered India in 1996 through a franchise agreement with VamBhartia Corp.

In Delhi. With the overwhelming success of the first outlet, the company opened another outlet in Delhi. By 2000, Domino's had outlets in all major cities in India. When Domino's entered India, the concept of home delivery was still in its nascent stages. It existed only in some major cities and was restricted to delivery by the friendly neighborhood fast food outlets. Eating out at 'branded' restaurants was more common.

To penetrate the Indian market, Domino's introduced an integrated home delivery system from a network of company outlets within 30 minutes of the order. Goutham Advani (Advani), Chief of Marketing, Domino's Pizza India, said, "What really worked its way into the Indian mind set was the promised 30-minute delivery." Domino's also offered compensation: Rs.30/- off the price tag if there was a delay in delivery. For the first 4 years in India, Domino's concentrated on its 'Delivery' strategy

Domino's Logistics Model

Analysts felt that Domino's took a cue from McDonald's supply chain model. However, they opened that the level of complexity in McDonald's system in India was not as high as that of Domino's. Commented Bhatia, "McDonald's operations are not as spread out as ours. They are in four cities while we are in 16.Centralizing wouldn't work on such a geographical scale. The logistics model adopted by Domino's offered some obvious benefits including lower transportation costs, cheaper procurement and economies of scale. Domino's had already cut out the duplication in procurement and processing of raw materials across each of the three commissaries.

The old model of self-contained commissaries had another disadvantage: adding new outlets did not translate into greater economies of scale. Bhatia planned to extend the model to other parts of the country as well. The commissary was to be located near the largest market in that region. Bhatia said, "Our roll-out began only after we mapped out our procurement strategy." Based on the agricultural map of India, Domino's looked McDonald's had one of the best logistics models in India. To maintain consistency and quality of its products, McDonald's shipped all the raw materials lettuce, patties et al to a cold storage close to the main market. Based on a daily demand schedule that was prepared a day in advance, the required amount of raw material was transported to individual outlets.

For the best product at the lowest cost. Thus, tomatoes would come from Bhubaneshwar, spices from the south, baby corn from Nepal (where it's 40% cheaper than in India) and vegetables from Sri Lanka. Similarly, Domino's India planned to extend its operations to Nepal, Sri Lanka and Dhaka. The company planned to establish a commissary in Sri Lanka, Domino's also identified specialty crops in each region. The commissary in that region was entrusted with the task of processing that specialty crop. For instance, the commissary for the eastern region in Kolkata was responsible for buying tomatoes, processing them and then sending them to all the other commissaries. Similarly, the northern commissary had to deliver pizza bases. This way, Domino's minimized duplication as well as the dangers of perishability. Once the new model was formalized, Bhatia planned to use Domino's 25 refrigerated truck s

To transport products for other companies on the same route. For instance, if an operator in Kochi (Kerala) needed to transport specialty cheese, he could use the Domino's fleet to transport his products. Said Bhatia, "Not too many people have refrigerated trucks in the country. And we can offer them quality service because we will be giving them standards we use for ourselves." Company sources said that enquiries from clients for such transport facilities had started coming in. Bhatia said he was in the process of selecting a person to head the logistics operation, which would be spun off as a separate profit centre. Bhatia seemed confident that the profit centre had the potential to bring in Rs 10 billion by 2006. However, he said the profit center would not be allowed to impede the growth of the pizza business, Domino's core operation. Only those deliveries that did not delay or de-route the truck would be considered.

Domino's hoped to lower its prices by saving from the logistics model and third-party transportation. In April 2000, Domino's announced a cut in pizza prices to Rs 49. Domino's was also targeting large corporate offices, railway stations, cinema halls and university campuses for faster growth. It had already established an outlet at Infosys corporate office in Bangalore and at three cinema halls - PVR in Delhi, Rex in Bangalore and New Empire in Kolkata. Domino's also classified its outlets into Super stores, Express stores and Regular stores.

Superstores were those, which generated high traffic and therefore had more counters than the regular outlets (the outlet in Churchgate, Mumbai).Express stores were those where people were expected to walk in and order rather than ask for home delivery (university campuses, offices or cinema halls).

Conclusion

Managing logistics and operations in a business is highly crucial to ensure that the company meet out the necessities and requirements of consumers on regular basis. As in the case we understand the need and importance of Domino''s new model of supply chain in India and how and why it is compared it with McDonald's supply chain model. In future Dominos have to focus more on its supply chain management as the number of its branches and overall business is increasing in India. They have to increase their operational efficiency and purchasing process.

Case Questions :

1. Briefly explain the need for Domino's to revamp its supply chain operations in India?

2. What are the benefits Domino's derived after the revamp.

3. Compare the supply chain models of Domino's and McDonald's. Which model is superior and why?

17. Flipkart Vs. Amazon'- Combat or Compromise?

A case Study in E- retailing

Learning Objectives:

i. To study how Indian e-commerce companies go back to their drawing table, brainstorm and rethink their current strategies and formulate new strategies to tackle the new challenges efficiently

ii. To study how the big cash advantage of Amazon over Flipkart made it able to catch up with other retailers as well as Flipkart.

iii. To study the journey of Amazon in India will going to be very tough considering the very unique buying behavior of Indian consumers, first thing that comes to customer's mind is discount, which is not the way it has happened in US, UK and other western countries?

iv. To study the Flipkart- Myntra deal because fashion and lifestyle is not only one of the largest categories in online retail in India

v. To study the model that Flipkart follows requires a large amount of investment and creates huge pressure in managing the logistics at the backend.

vi. To study the Flipkart competition from some of the brick-and-mortar retail companies apart from the online players that have begun to strengthen their online sales channels.

vii. To study the challenges that Amazon is going to face as it is set to enter Indian Online food delivery market form August 2020

Synopsis:

Considering how popular both Amazon and Flipkart in India, more and more people are opting to shop online compared to offline.

Flipkart was established in 2007 by Sachin Bansal and Binny Bansal, both alumni of the Indian Institute of Technology Delhi. They worked for Amazon.com before quitting and founding their own company. The store started with selling books and in 2010 branched out to selling CDs, DVDs, mobile phones & accessories, cameras, computers, computer accessories and peripherals, pens & office supplies, other electronic items such as home appliances, kitchen appliances, personal care gadgets, health care products.

When the company, Amazon launched Amazon.in, its online marketplace in India, in June 2013, it had just 100 sellers across two categories — books and movies, and television shows. Amazon now has a base of 5,000 sellers and a selection of more than 15 million* products across 25 categories including music, video games, toys, home goods, luggage, jewelry and beauty products.

Amazon has been active on other fronts, too. For instance, it took the lead among online retailers in India to introduce **same-day and next-day deliveries**. To reach its customers faster, Amazon is now running a pilot for last-mile delivery by partnering with neighborhood mom-and-pop stores.

Amazon has big cash advantage over Flipkart hence it was able to catch up with other retailers as well as Flipkart. Jeff Bezos keeps pumping millions of dollars every year to Indian market even though they are not making profit as of now. He has good vision and understands that capturing the market is more important rather than making profit in the initial years.

Among the Indian online retailers, companies like Jabong, Snapdeal and Myntra have shown promise and could be in a position to give a tough fight to Flipkart.

The case details:

The e-tailing market in India might have been a late starter, but it is now showing signs of growth. According to Internet and Mobile Association of India, e-commerce market in India is expected to grow to $200* billion by 2020. Experts say that companies like Flipkart have been instrumental in creating excitement for online shopping in India. With its catchy television commercials, easy-to-use services and popular product range, Flipkart has undoubtedly set the ground on fire.

With the Indian e-commerce market showing signs of taking off, global players have also started warming up to the opportunities here. Amazon recently announced its entry into the Indian market, while eBay has established its third development in Bangalore and plans to hire 1,000 IT professionals by 2016.

Flipkart went live in 2007 with the objective of making books easily available to anyone who had internet access. Today, they're present across various categories including movies, music, games, mobiles, cameras, computers, healthcare and personal products, home appliances and electronics, stationery, perfumes, toys, apparels, shoes – and still counting! Be it their path- breaking services like Cash on Delivery, a 30-day replacement policy, EMI options, free shipping - and of course the great prices that they offer, everything they do revolves around their obsession with providing their customers a memorable online shopping experience. Then there's their dedicated Flipkart delivery partners who work round the clock to personally make sure the packages reach on time.

The two companies are in the same business and there will

be similarities in the services or features each launches. Few months before Amazon launched its 'marketplace' in India under the Amazon.in name, Flipkart launched its version of the marketplace. In July, it first announced its payments brand 'Pay Zippy' for online merchants and customers seeking fast, hassle-free and safe payment options. Given the critical mass of transactions Flipkart controls - about 100,000 a day - the company is betting that it has the volumes to lay the foundation of what will be a profitable business. It is much like how Amazon bet on web server and storage services and made a successful business out of it. In December, Flipkart launched a one-day guaranteed delivery service, just five days after Amazon announced it.

Flipkart was established in 2007 by Sachin Bansal and Binny Bansal, both alumni of the Indian Institute of Technology Delhi. They worked for Amazon.com before quitting and founding their own company. Initially they used word of mouth marketing to popularize their company. A few months later, the company sold its first book on flipkart.com – 'John Wood's Leaving Microsoft to Change the World'. Flipkart broke even in March 2010 and claims to have had at least 100% growth every quarter since its founding. The store started with selling books and in 2010 branched out to selling CDs, DVDs, mobile phones & accessories, cameras, computers, computer accessories and peripherals, pens & office supplies, other electronic items such as home appliances, kitchen appliances, personal care gadgets, health care products.

Entry of Amazon.com as Amazon.in in India

The past year has been action-packed for Amazon in India. The country's online retail market is around $3 billion at present, but it is expected to cross $50 billion by 2020 — and the globalonline retail giant is gearing up to play a dominant role in the sector.

While Amazon has been compelled to adopt different a business model in India to comply with foreign direct investment (FDI) regulations — India does not permit FDI for online companies that have their own inventory — the ramp-up of its operations in the country has been the fastest globally for the Seattle-based $75 billion firm. When the company launched Amazon.in, its online marketplace in India, in June 2013, it had just 100 sellers across two categories — books and movies, and television shows. Amazon now has a base of 5,000 sellers and a selection of more than 15 million* products across 25 categories including music, video games, toys, home goods, luggage, jewelry and beauty products. According to media reports, industry estimates put Amazon's India sales at around $200 million.

Amazon has been active on other fronts, too. For instance, it took the lead among online retailers in India to introduce **same-day and next-day deliveries**. To reach its customers faster, Amazon is now running a pilot for last-mile delivery by partnering with neighborhood mom-and-pop stores. Amazon also has two fulfillment centers in the country — one on the outskirts of Mumbai, and the other in Bangalore, each about 150,000 square feet. These two centers stock products across several categories from sellers using "fulfillment by Amazon" – a service in which Amazon takes complete care of packing, shipping and delivery of the sellers' products.

"India is a very important market for Amazon globally. We are committed to India and are here for the long term," says Amit Agarwal, vice president and country manager of Amazon India. "We take it as an article of faith that customers will shop on Amazon.in only until the very moment they find a better customer experience elsewhere. It's truly 'Day 1' for us, and we are committed to aggressively investing over the long term and relentlessly focusing on raising the bar for the online shopping experience in India."

Now with the entry of Amazon in India (www.amazon.in), Indian e-commerce market is expected to take new shapes on many fronts. Looking at the already crowded Indian e-commerce market and considering the size, scale and deep pockets of Amazon, it would be very interesting to see which way does the market make a shift?

Back in Feb 2013, when for the first time people got to know that Amazon is planning to set-up its online presence in India, All experts and stalwarts were favoring inorganic way for Amazon to enter into Indian market. Being an acquisitive company by approach, there were almost no arguments on that.

Against the expectations of all and surprising everyone, Amazon chooses organic way to enter into Indian market. They always had this "Make versus Buy" decision option with them, but paying a very big cheque to acquire versus throwing a part of that money to learn the rope at their own, it seems like by going with the latter option, they actually played a master stroke.

Keeping Indian e-commerce players busy in the anticipation that it will follow it's traditionally followed inorganic approach to enter or expand in new territory and consequently making them work on increasing their valuations, it all seems like a part of very well executed plan. Now Indian e-commerce companies need to go back to their drawing table, brainstorm and rethink their current strategies and formulate new strategies to tackle the new challenges efficiently.

As far as Amazon is concerned, no one has doubts about their capabilities. Their brand value and track record of continuously coming-up with new innovations to surprise their customers make them hot favorite among masses. From a sky view, it seems like things are very well placed for Amazon but let's not forget the intricacies that are there in Indian e-commerce market. For Amazon, it would be interesting to see, do they have the minimum required knowledge to operate in Indian market? How efficiently will they handle logistic and supply chain issues? The thing that is favoring their organic move is the strong database which they have earned with www. junglee. com and in such a case it becomes very important for them to leverage on that, else their journey in India will going to be very tough considering the very unique buying behavior of Indian consumers. Another challenge they will have to face is the mentality of Indians about online shopping. With the thought of online shopping, first thing that comes to customer's mind is discount, which is not the way it has happened in US, UK and other western countries?

After learning both the sides of coin for Amazon, it is definite that Amazon's entry will certainly shake-up the e-commerce market in India. Flipkart had foreseen this move coming and their latest acquisition of www.letsbuy.com will definitely strengthen their position. For others, a lot is there to do. With the entry of Amazon, to survive and sustain, we foresee e-commerce industry to move towards consolidation. Only time will tell what exactly will happen in Indian e-commerce industry but it would be really interesting to see how Indian players take-up this challenge?

The Flipkart- Myntra deal* is important because fashion and lifestyle is not only one of the largest categories in online retail in India — it accounts for more than 25% of the market and is expected to increase to as much as 40% — it also has among the best margins. While margins in branded apparel can go up to 35%, for in-house brands it can be as high as 60%. The companies are looking to increase their combined market share in this category from 50% at present to around 70%. Flipkart has already committed to investing upwards of $100 million in the combined fashion business over the next 12 to 18 months.

Who will grab the biggest pie?

With the entry of global giants like Amazon and eBay into India, experts say that Flipkart will now have to really pull up its socks. "Strategic players like Amazon and eBay will play out a long-term strategy within the constraints imposed on them," AshishBhinde, executive director (digital media and technology), Avendus Capital said in a report in Live Mint. "However, this level of capital does give Flipkart significant firepower to extend its lead to a level that makes it more challenging for Amazon and others to catch up."

Among the Indian online retailers, companies like Jabong, Snap deal and Myntra have shown promise and could be in a position to give a tough fight to Flipkart. The model that Flipkart follows requires a large amount of investment and creates huge pressure in managing the logistics at the backend. If any other e-commerce company can find an innovative way of reducing the operational costs, it could be in a more competitive position, suggests an expert.

Apart from the online players, Flipkart also faces competition from some of the brick-and-mortar retail companies that have begun to strengthen their online sales channels.

Conclusions:

The e-retailing market in India is late starter, but it is now showing signs of growth. The e-commerce market in India is expected to grow to $200* billion by the end of 2020.

Flipkart was the first prominent marketplace to start online sales in India which started in the year 2007. Amazon stepped into Indian market as late as 2013, while eBay has established its third development in Bangalore and plans to hire 1,000 IT professionals by 2016.

Among the Indian online retailers, companies like Jabong, Snapdeal and Myntra have shown promise and could be in a position to give a tough fight to Flipkart. The model that Flipkart follows requires a large amount of investment and creates huge pressure in managing the logistics at the backend. If any other e-commerce company can find an innovative way of reducing the operational costs, it could be in a more competitive position, suggests an expert.

Looking at the already crowded Indian e-commerce market and considering the size, scale and deep pockets of Amazon, it would be very interesting to see which way does the market make a shift?

Case Questions:

1.1.   How well designed marketing mix (Business Model) can help the Flipkart to sustain the marketing challenges.

1.2.   What kind of marketing innovation is required by the local Flipkart to fight the tough competition put up by global giant Amazon.com?

1.3.   Having a status of market 'pioneer' can Flipkart retain its position as market 'leader' also?

Q.4.   Will the pilot by Amazon named last-mile delivery to reach its customers faster, by partnering with neighborhood mom-and-pop stores be an advantage over the other e-retailers?

Q.5.   How successful the multinational giants like Amazon, e-bay will be to understand the mentality of Indians about online shopping. With the thought of online shopping, first thing that comes to customer's mind is discount, which is not the way it has happened in US, UK and other western countries?

18. The 'Wal Kart' of India

A Case Study on Walmart-Flip Kart merger

Learning Objectives:

The aim of the paper is facilitate,

- ➢ To understand the entry strategies of MNC's for businesses into the International Market.

- ➢ To study the scenario of the market and the competition prevailing due to new entrants in the market.

- ➢ It provides us to frame out the strategy to explore the untapped Emerging market and gain the profits out of it.

- ➢ To provide insights on how to become a threat for the competitors into the market by utilizing the resources of their competitors.

Synopsis:

The case here discusses about the strategies being framed by the retail giants to occupy and bring in stiff competition for the purpose of staying for long into the Market. All it started with the takeover strategy by Wal-Mart of Flipkart with 77% stake in it. This news broke out like fire and created fear in minds of few and some got ratified with it. Everything revolved around, will this deal prove to be the blessing or curse for the Indian retail or e-commerce industry. The study here provides an in depth knowledge about how to explore the opportunities in the untapped market and how to make it lucrative for the other company to accept the deal.

Introduction:

US retail giant Wal-Mart has signed a definitive agreement to acquire a 77 per cent stake in India's largest e-commerce marketplace "Flipkart" with an investment of around $16 billion, making it the largest transaction in history of the online retail space globally.

The deal, which wiped away $10 billion of Wal-Mart's market capitalization as investors reacted negatively in early morning trade on the New York Stock Exchange, stands out for several exits. The biggest was Sachin Bansal selling his entire 5.96 per cent stake for $1.23 billion and parting ways with Flipkart that he had founded in 2007 along with friend from IIT, Binny Bansal (not related). Sachin was nowhere around at the Flipkart campus when the Wal-Mart top team led by CEO Doug McMillon addressed employees in a town hall meeting Wednesday evening.

Another significant exit is that of Soft Bank, the largest investor in Flipkart. In a strange coincidence, the deal, valuing Flipkart at $20.8 billion, was announced to the world by Soft Bank Chief Executive Masayoshi Son in a webinar with investor's hours before Wal-Mart did so. He also confirmed that Soft Bank would get about $4 billion from its $2.5-billion investment in Flipkart last August.

Flipkart's valuation at $20.8 billion is a 75 per cent increase over its previous valuation in the range of $11-12 billion last August. Out of the $16-billion investment, Wal-Mart will put in $2 billion in new equity funding, while the rest will be utilized to acquire stakes of existing investors in the Bengaluru-based company.

In a statement issued on Wednesday, Wal-Mart said it would eventually look at the public listing of Flipkart as a majority-owned subsidiary though the company did not share a timeline for this. The Bentonville, Arkansas-headquartered Company said the deal would be closed later in the current calendar year, subject to regulatory approvals. While the deal was being watched by world leaders, back home there were voices of protest. The RSS economic wing called it Wal-Mart's backdoor entry into India, and traders' association CAIT argued the deal would "vitiate Indian e-commerce".

Retail majors, including Kishore Biyani of the Future group, too, watched the deal with interest and told Business Standard that strategic deals with online players would be the future of retail in India. The deal, advised by JP Morgan from the Wal-Mart side and Goldman Sachs for Flipkart, would bring in the largest piece of FDI into India. This would give Wal-Mart access to the fast-growing online retail space in the country. More than anything else, this would help Wal-Mart fight its battle with rival Amazon, which lags behind Flipkart in terms of gross merchandise value (GMV). But the Indian authorities are already asking Wal-Mart and Flipkart about the tax liabilities post the mega transaction. According to global research and analyst firm Forrester, India's e-commerce sector hit $19.2 billion in sales in 2017 and is expected to grow to $73 billion by 2022, at a compound annual growth rate of 30.62 per cent.

After the US and China, India is expected to be the next big market for online retail and is the last large, untapped market globally. "India is one of the most attractive retail markets in the world, given its size and growth rate, and our investment is an opportunity to partner with the company that is leading transformation of e-commerce in the market," said Wal-Mart'sMcMillon."Ourinvestment will benefit India providing quality, affordable goods for customers, while creating new skilled jobs and fresh opportunities for small suppliers, farmers and women entrepreneurs," he added.

Flipkart and Wal-Mart also said they were in discussions with other investors to participate in the round without offering any details of who these additional investors could be. Insiders say, Alphabet, the parent company of Google, has shown interest to invest in the online retail firm and is in discussion with them. While further investments in Flipkart could bring down Wal-Mart's overall stake in the company, it said that it would retain "clear majority ownership".

After the deal is closed, Binny Bansal, co-founder and Group CEO at Flipkart, will continue to hold the same position. "Wal-Mart is the ideal partner for the next phase of our journey, and we look forward to working together in the years ahead to bring our strengths and learning's in retail and ecommerce to the fore," said Binny Bansal. "This investment is of immense importance for India and will help fuel our ambition to deepen our connection with buyers and sellers and to create the next wave of retailinIndia."Flipkart's second largest shareholder, Tiger Global Management, will sell a large portion of its shares and retain a small holding in the company,

Wal-Mart management reposed strong faith in the existing leadership at Flipkart and its subsidiaries including Myntra and PhonePe. Wal-Mart said Tencent, Tiger Global and Microsoft will continue to be its strategic and technology partners. Experts say Wal-Mart still has an uphill task of competing with Amazon, which it has struggled to do on its own home turf   in the US. Wal-Mart can utilize its sourcing and retail powers to aid Flipkart's efficiency; it still needed to come up with a product that can match Amazon's Prime loyalty programme. While the deal gave Wal-Mart access to India, which is the largest market outside of the US and China, its stock could continue to see pressure from investors post the deal. Unlike Amazon's investors who reward the company for diverting profits to win in new markets, Wal-Mart's stock is significantly undervalued and they'd have to answer a lot more questions about their India investment considering Flipkart was still making losses,. The company's stock was down 5.3 per cent before the market opened in New York, and subsequently started recovering.

The Aftermath:

The story of how two young men grew a small online bookstore called Flipkart into an ecommerce giant is one that Indian entrepreneurs will remember for years, even as the country's largest conglomerates possibly regret missing out on it.

Wal-Mart's $16-billion acquisition of a 77 per cent stake in India's largest online marketplace is the world's biggest ecommerce deal. While this proves that Indian businesses are capable of offering stellar exits to investors, it also shows that the country has not been able to sustain local corporate champions.

The Flipkart-Wal-Mart deal, entrepreneurs and investors hope will be the trigger for domestic companies to look deeper into India's internet ecosystem, including at financial technology, health technology, and artificial intelligence businesses. "This is a big wake-up call for large Indian corporate houses. The fault is theirs for having stood on the sidelines," said an investor in a consumer internet startup, declining to be identified. "Indian businessmen looked at the internet ecosystem with skepticism while foreigners saw value in it."

Among Flipkart's top investors were Japanese internet conglomerate Softbank, South African media group Naspers, Chinese messaging app We Chat's parent company Tencent and US technology giant Microsoft. All of these have now exited Flipkart, fetching handsome returns from the Wal-Mart deal.

Even if Flipkart may have become too big for Indian companies to back, investors say there were several other opportunities in recent years for local corporate giants to participate in the country's commerce boom.

Moreover, backing internet companies across sectors would have been a good investment thesis, not just in terms of financial returns but also as a means to adapt and learn from emerging technology to stay relevant, say investors and entrepreneurs (Supported by Source: TRACXN).

"Some of the top 10 Fortune 500 companies in the US are tech companies. In the next 10 years from India, how will that happen? Other industries are equally important but the market cap will come from tech companies," said K Ganesh, founder of startup incubator Growth Story. "Those who invested in Flipkart are those who took the bold bets instead of criticizing valuations and unit economics. Unless one takes bold bets how will you play the market later?"

Increase in Capital Flow:

The Flipkart-Wal-Martdeal is likely to increase the flow of capital into the domestic ecosystem, as limited partners globally reopen their purses with renewed confidence in one of the fastest-growing developing markets. Limited partners are investors in venture capital and other funds. This expected surge in capital, however, would play a limited role in stoking interest among individuals to start businesses, unlike in 2014-2015 when increased flow brought with it a surge in start up formation, said experts.

About 13,685 start ups were formed in India in 2015, of which about 20% were ecommerce companies, as India's internet ecosystem undertook a massive cleanup both in terms of quality of businesses and quantity of capital invested, that number nosedived to 2,671.

Exit Options:

Flipkart's sale is also expected to give start up founders theconfidence to go against the tide, with the deal establishing

India as a potentially hot market for more such investment exits.

"The valuation outcome that Flipkart has garnered (of nearly $21 billion) has blown past even that of an IPO. This is a signal for entrepreneurs to not rush into an IPO because there are better exits if one disrupts the market enough, does not cede ground and attempts to gain market share whatever be the cost,". "Value does not lie only in having a profitable IPO-led business. Flipkart has shown that."

The deal marks the largest exit for investors in India's technology landscape. Investors cashing out of Flipkart are expected to collectively fetch about $14 billion when the deal completes, answering long-held doubts on if investments in Indian start ups would yield results.

Investors believe that the deal marks the first step towards the creation of a more mature market where one can see more exits spread across a larger number of companies and consistently so, over the next few years. "If you look at a market like Israel, over the past five years, they have consistently had exits in technology companies cumulatively amounting to over $40 billion across 300 VC- and PE-backed firms,"

Of Angels and Mafias:

The $500-million bounty that Flipkart employees are in for from the Wal-Mart deal presents a potential bounty for the larger ecosystem as well. About 100 current and former Flipkart employees with ESOPs are now estimated to be worth more than $1 million. A good part of that money could flow back into the start up ecosystem as some of these now wealthy individuals may turn investors and entrepreneurs themselves.

Industry executives see the Flipkart-Wal-Mart deal as a turning point for India's angel investing ecosystem, even if just $100 million from liquidated ESOPs is invested back into start ups "The Flipkart Angel Group is one of the more powerful emerging angel investor groups in the ecosystem."

The emergence of such a large capital pool is particularly timely given the steady dip in angel and seed investments that the ecosystem has witnessed over the last three years. Data from Venture Intelligence show a slow recovery in the first four months of 2018 with $62 million in angel investments.

Flipkart's acquisition is likely to hasten that pace and bring the zing back in angel investing, say experts. Former Flipkart employees such as Sujeet Kumar of logistics firm Udaan and Curefit founder Mukesh Bansal are expected to be some of the biggest beneficiaries of cashing out from Flipkart. That's apart from Sachin Bansal, who is exiting the company he founded with a $1 billion harvest from selling his shares to Wal-Mart. Mukesh Bansal's Curefit is one of the foremost examples of the so-called 'Flipkart Mafia,' with the fitness chain counting Myntra CEO Ananth Narayanan, Flipkart cofounder Binny Bansal and CEO Kalyan Krishnamurthy as angel investors.

Mukesh Bansal was a founding member of online fashion retailer Myntra, which Flipkart bought in 2014. With over 200 start ups founded by former Flipkart employees and over $200 million invested in these startups, this 'Flipkart Mafia' is set to further grow, leaving behind it a far richer ecosystem of start ups, investors and serial entrepreneurs.

Wal-Mart's Low Pricing Model Worries Sellers:

Sellers on Flipkart are already apprehensive that Wal-Mart will bring its global everyday low pricing business model on general merchandise to the marketplace, indulging in deep discounting,

However, the deal could also give Flipkart an improved supply chain and make it more process-oriented, which will help it to compete with Amazon, some sellers said. The real fight will be in food retailing, where 100% foreign direct investment is allowed and Amazon has government approval to start this business. Although India doesn't allow online marketplaces such as Flipkart and Amazon to influence prices of products sold on their platforms, sellers have objected to units of these ecommerce companies selling their private labels at discounts.

The 'Every Day Low Costs, Every Day Low Prices' offer, which has made Wal-Mart the world's top retailer, could add to the competitive pressure on smaller online sellers and drive them out of business. They fear getting squeezed between the two giants — the Wal-Mart-Flipkart combine and Amazon — even though consumers will benefit. "Wal-Mart has global purchase power that gives it a big advantage in terms of costs," said VishwasShringi, cofounder at Voylla Retail, a large fashion and lifestyle products seller on online marketplaces including Flipkart.

"They can come and disrupt the entire market with their 'everyday low pricing offer.' This will definitely put pressure on sellers as they would now compete with Wal-Mart predatory pricing, which is impossible to beat." An electronics sellerfears the Wal-Mart-Flipkart deal will once again bring back insanity into discounting, at least in the short run. "Deep discounts had become limited to only major sales. But the deal may increase discounting and would also sway Amazon into it. This may happen for at least the first few months since Wal-Mart would want to show its supremacy," said the seller, requesting anonymity.

Wal-Mart May Step Up India Sourcing for Global Market:

Wal-Mart will likely step up sourcing from India for its global operations as the Flipkart acquisition gives it access to the huge supplier base of the ecommerce company. The US-based retailer currently sources goods worth over a "couple of billion" dollars, such as apparel, generic medicines and handicrafts, from Indian suppliers such as Welspun and Dr Reddy's for its stores in the US, UK, Canada and South America,

Wal-Mart's sourcing from India is still small compared with that from China, which ships some $50 billion worth of goods to the company's stores, but the combination of its Best Price cash and carry business and Flipkart is now expected to help boost India's contribution. The bigger base of suppliers from Flipkart will offer it more opportunities to source for its retail outlets abroad, while also allowing the suppliers a wider exposure to overseas markets. While Flipkart had an association with eBay to take sellers global as eBay cashed out and decided to relaunch its website.

Wal-Mart said it would support small business and 'Make in India' through direct procurement as well as provide increased opportunities for exports through global sourcing and ecommerce. Analysts said the India market opportunity for Wal-Mart will in fact be meatier than that from building a larger supply chain to source goods for global markets. "Nothing was stopping them from sourcing (from India) anyways. Wal-Mart might increase it a little bit more.

They are going to bring a lot of products from outside to Indian customers, which they were not able to sell earlier. They will now channel that in India through Flipkart." Wal-Mart has over 20 Best Price cash and carry outlets in India. In fiscal 2017, the India unit posted revenue of Rs 3,641 crore, of which two-thirds came from sales of food and groceries.

Wal-Mart's sourcing and negotiating power for Best Price is what Flipkart is looking for, said Meena, adding that the Indian retailer could "get an edge on food and private" labels with the deal. "Between cash and carry business and Flipkart, Wal-Mart will focus more on India. They have the backend systems and expertise in large-scale sourcing. They will focus on expanding the 100 million (Flipkart) customers". Wal-Mart is also looking to consolidate its India operations in Bengaluru, where Flipkart is based.

Wal-Mart Opens a New Front in Global Battle with Amazon:

Wal-Mart's acquisition of a controlling stake in Flipkart has raised several questions on the future of India's largest online retailer

For fiscal year 2016-17, Flipkart reported a 29% increase in revenue to Rs19,854 crore, but the report had two red flags. The first was that revenue growth had slowed from 50% in the prior year, and the second was that Flipkart's loss had increased 68% to Rs 8,771 crore. In spite of that, Tiger Global, Flipkart's largest investor until recently, priced the company at nearly $18 billion when it invested $424 million in it in January, an astounding rise in value for a company started in 2007 with Rs 6 Lakh in capital. Wal-Mart is paying $16 billion for 77% of Flipkart, valuing the company at nearly $21 billion.

It is no secret that Wal-Mart has been eyeing the Indian market for a while, recognizing the potential for growth in retailing here. But attempts to enter this market for much of the last few decades have not been successful. At the start of 2018, Wal-Mart owned 21 stores in India, a small profile for a market the size of India. The most direct explanation for Wal-Mart's acquisition of Flipkart is that it gives the company a significant foothold in India's online retail market, and perhaps benefits Wal-Mart's brick-and-mortar retail investments in the country.

Given that Flipkart is losing substantial amounts already, the potential for increased income is minimal, at least in the near-term. You would need a big boost from the combination to justify the premium. It is, therefore, no surprise that many observers, looking at the deal standing alone, and given that Wal-Mart is more likely to be investing money into the deal rather than taking money out, have concluded that Wal-Mart is paying too much for too little.

A simpler explanation for the Wal-Mart gambit and it has its roots in a global battle that Wal-Mart is involved in with Amazon. Amazon is the most fearsome competitor on the face of the earth, and has been successful at laying to waste entire businesses. In fact, when Amazon announces plans to enter a new business), the market routinely knocks down the values of competitors in that business by 10% or more. In the brick and-mortar retail business in the United States, Amazon's conquest is almost complete, with Wal-Mart remaining its only major rival.

In fact, Wal-Mart is one of the few companies that has been able to go head-to-head against Amazon in online retailing in the US, with its acquisition of Wayfair, an online retailer. Wal-Mart has been watching Amazon's aggressive investment in India with trepidation, concerned that Amazon will make its control of Indian online retailing complete by either driving Flipkart out of business or acquiring it, putting at risk Wal-Mart's long-term plan of opening brick-and-mortar retail stores in the country.

Put differently, Wal-Mart's acquisition of Flipkart fundamentally seems to be a defensive maneuver, where Wal-Mart is engaging Amazon in India by supplying badly needed capital to Flipkart to continue in business, with the promise of more if needed. Wal-Mart's war with Amazon is fought on many fronts and in much geography, and ceding a market as big as India to Amazon would set Wal-Mart back in that global battle. Viewed in that perspective, where you have hundreds of billions of dollars in play, a multibillion premium paid on an acquisition is penny change. This battle among multinational behemoths also explains why Google is also a player in this acquisition, since it, too, fears Amazon's entry into its business space.

This acquisition will open the floodgates to even more intense competition in the online retail space in India, and both Wal-Mart and Amazon will lose more money in the near-term as a consequence. The beneficiaries, though, will be Indian consumers who will wake up to better deals, lower shipping costs, and expedited service, as the two giants open their pockets. Let the good times roll!

What Wal-Mart Will Do Next After Buying in India, Selling in UK:

Wal-Mart has agreed to cede control of its British business to a competitor and spend $16billion to acquire Flipkart. The sun never sets on Wal-Mart Inc.'s empire, thanks to its network of stores across five continents. But in the span of 10 days, chief executive Doug McMillon has begun dramatically redrawing the retailer's map, and there's likely more to come as it places bets to remain on top .In less than two weeks, Wal-Mart has agreed to cede control of its British business to a competitor and spend $16 billion to acquire India's e-commerce leader in its biggest-ever deal, fending off Amazon.com Inc. The wheeling and dealing show how McMillon is focusing on high-potential markets like China and India, finding partners to help it battle online and cutting loose middling businesses. He's got more work to do, though, and subpar markets like Brazil and Japan might be next on his list.

Wal-Mart's far-flung international units don't get much attention, but they're important as a source of cash, management talent and ideas that percolate into its core U.S. operations. Sales growth outside the U.S. once topped more than 10 percent annually, adjusted for currency moves, but it's less than half that now as sluggish economies, store closures and fierce competition have taken their toll.

Those pressures -- combined with a U.S. e-commerce business that continues to spill red ink and higher labor expenses from this year's wage hike -- have forced McMillon into hard choices. Some, like selling the British Asda stores, were welcomed by Wall Street, but Wednesday's deal got a rude welcome from investors, who raised concerns about Flipkart's steep losses and asked whether Wal-Mart's cash would be better spent elsewhere. S&P Global Ratings said the heavy spending to compete with Amazon could threaten Wal-Mart's pristine credit rating.McMillon defended the Flipkart deal to analysts, saying it was a unique opportunity. He's certainly mindful of past missteps abroad, such as his 2011 decision to buy an unprofitable, second-tier online marketplace in China that's forced the company to play catch-up to Alibaba -- the Amazon of China—ever since. Wal-Mart's international reach sprawls across 6,360 stores in about two dozen countries from Argentina to Zambia. Many were acquired during a buying spree from 1999 to 2009, but that era of aggressive flag-planting is long over. Today the international business accounts for less than one-quarter of Wal-Mart's total revenue, down from nearly 30 percent five years ago. That share will decline further after Wal-Mart's decision to merge its Asda business in the U.K. with Sainsbury Plc, retreating from a market that was once its shining star abroad. Other moves are expected to follow, as the Asda sale "was the first volley" in a broader reshuffle of Wal-Mart's global holdings, said Mark Stoeckle, portfolio manager of the Adams Diversified Equity Fund, which owns Wal-Mart shares. Stoeckle and other investors were encouraged when Wal-Mart's finance chief, Brett Biggs, said in October that he's "open to taking action" to simplify operations. Getting leaner should help Wal-Mart devote more focus and firepower to its escalating battle with Amazon, which is trying to crack categories like food and apparel, long Wal-Mart strongholds. Acquiring e-commerce start up Jet.com two years ago has helped, but the Flip kart deal suggests that future moves will likely come outside the U.S.

Conclusions:

India has always been an option for the struggling or the winning brands to explore more opportunities, likewise Wal- Mart too tried its hands on experience in the Indian e-commerce industry by reflecting its strategy of reviving the Flipkart again, though wanted to occupy the market share. The wars of the brands created an opportunity for India too to revive again in the e-commerce market with a bang. Though the hustle of the brands would make the defeat the production sector of India too but the accessibility to standardized products for Indian customers will increase. It is difficult to say whether the deal will only be profitable for the Indian retailers but it can confidently be derived that Wal-mart would prove to be the stiff competitor for Amazon.

Outcomes

Every coin has two sides, in the same way the takeover or the tug of war of the two retail giants would even be profitable or it can be unfavorable too. The deal of Flipkart and Wal-Mart can be favorable to some extent for the Indian retailers and consumers in a way, can generate employment opportunities, accessibility to the standardized products, better market, more varieties, new products and innovations, but then to some extent would defeat the production of Indian goods and services in the Indian market. The EDLP strategy of Wal-Mart would kill the small online retailers in India. Therefore it's the wakeup call for the industrialists in India to explore the untapped market of India, in spite it being targeted by the foreign companies.

Case Questions:

Q1. Do you think that Wal-Mart is hell bent on entering the

Indian Retail market in spite of restrictions imposed by Government of India on Foreign companies investing in Multi Brand Retail Market (Single Brand has no such restrictions)?And this is the main reason of 77% takeover bid of Flip Kart?(Support with logical reasons)

Q2. Wal-Mart has been in India since nearly a decade in B2-B Market and in establishing its supply chain Technology projects at the back office of many Indian Ecommerce companies. Now once the Merger/take over is cleared by the competition committee of India Wal-Mart could use the existing outlets of Flipkart to exploit its own Multi brand products in India through its FLIP KART outlets since strategically they have decided to Keep Flip Karts Business and net works independent even after It gets all clearances. Of what specific interest is this merger to Indian Retail Market?

Q3. Wal-Mart has many class action suits pending against it challenging its Work practices and exploitation of its work force of issues related to human work environment and discrimination against communities How do you rate this possibility in India with its glaring un employment and social issues.? Will this takeover be a blessing in disguise for Indian e-commerce market?

19. Intelligent path of modern business
The world of NETFLIX"

A Case Study on Social Media Apps and their impact

Learning objectives;

➢ Learning incentivizes autonomous decision-making by employees to create business enhancement and encourage merit.

➢ To understand and learn about how Netflix platforms exchange knowledge freely, widely and deliberately.

➢ Training and learning of the business deals with the delivery of internet access to its clients, the downloading of videos and TV shows over the phone and the faxing of DVDs.

➢ Understanding on Job and capacity requirements, fair pay arrangements, a clear choice for non-performers, flexible severance payments, the promise of wages and equity balances, etc.

Synopsis;

Transactions of the business is nothing but the culture of an organization — including its common ideals, principles, practices, and people — it is something rather intangible that acts as a basis for enhancing company development and success, and many organizations are failing to behave. However, businesses such as NETFLIX have created an incentive to build a high-performance organizational community. The very last area addressed in this case is how NETFLIX successfully embraced the transition taking place in the globe. This involves the positive adoption and introduction of technical improvements, while at the same time meeting consumer needs and demands

Introduction:

Organizational culture is nothing but the philosophy behind an organization- which includes its shared values, beliefs, norms, and its people. It is something which is rather intangible but acts like a supporting pillar for organizational success and achievements. But many companies fail to act sensibly to build its own unique identity- its culture. However, companies like NETFLIX has made an ace in setting a high performance organizational culture through its unique practices (let's not call them policies). It believes in offering its employees with utmost freedom and flexibility to work with minimal formalization. It thrives to establish a complete adult culture and summarize its working in one simple line 'Act in NETFLIX's best interest'. Simple yet so deep and thoughtful.

Netflix was incepted when its founder Reed Hastings saw an opportunity in DVD business while solving a simple math problem. And from there, the idea has grown and became a company with a net worth of $61.6 billion. The company deals in providing to its customers with subscription service streaming movies and TV episodes over the Internet and sending DVDs by mail. The case focuses on the how NETFLIX has carved a niche against all odds and came out as a warrior during the times when companies were facing the dotcom crises. The employment and hiring criteria, competitive compensation plans, straight-forward approach for non-performers, attractive severance packages, option to choose a mix between salary and equity, etc. are some of the broad areas discussed in the case. It was not easy for the company to stand erect in front of competitors like Amazon, Blockbuster, etc. But the strategies adopted by NETFLIX to keep its customer happy and satisfied, to retain its talent, and to accept the competitors' challenges, has made it even more stronger and tougher.

The final area that has been covered under the case is how effectively NETFLIX has accepted the change taking place in the external environment. It includes accepting the technological changes and implement it smoothly while keeping a balance between customers' needs and demands.

Netflix Business Model:

Netflix was founded in 1997 by Reed Hastings, who first conceived of a subscription-based online movie rental business when he was charged with the late fee of $40 for renting the movie Apollo 13 from Blockbuster. The idea then converted into a bigger dream and resulted in the introduction of the company called, NETFLIX. Netflix is one of its kind, dealing in renting unlimited movies (then, in DVD format) to its subscribers at monthly fee of $19.95 (then), with requests for the titles available over the internet.(It is important to note that erstwhile, DVD format was adopted as the standard format for watching the movies.)The business model adopted by the company was very simple, here customers were allowed to rent three movies through the mail at a time and can keep the movies with them as long as they want without incurring any late fee charges. Whenever customers want to order any other movie, they created a queue on the company website (Netflix. com) in their own preferential manner. Once a customer return one movie, the next movie in the queue automatically mailed to the customers. Postage charges for the both the sides were paid by Netflix itself.

How Netflix Business Model Succeeded?

- Firstly, Netflix aimed to cover its fixed cost by attracting the mass customers. In order to fulfil the demand of every customer and at the same time engage those who tend to cancel their subscription, Netflix offered a comprehensive collection of movie titles that were readily available on demand. This helped the company in preserving its customer base, thus covering its fixed cost.

- Secondly, Netflix ensured the minimum waiting time for the customer through its excellent and wide coverage of Delivery Services. And to serve the purpose, it leased the shipping centres in proximity with the customer population. This move helped it to deliver DVDs in one business day to 95% of its customers which ultimately resulted into grabbing customer loyalty and trust.

- Thirdly, in order to make itself more customer-friendly, Netflix facilitated its customer with an ease to access available titles and navigation through its website. The website so designed aimed at making the customer experience more realistic and interactive. Easy navigation, customer recommendation system with an autonomy to suggest their preferences, raising a platform for customers to share their reviews about the movies, and the use of computer algorithms to identify the movies which a customer might like to watch were some of the features available on the website. This step helped Netflix to share a strong relationship with its customers and increased customer satisfaction.

Strategies for Facing Challenges and Competitors:

Once initiated, Netflix never looked back and continued to expand its customer base. In the year 2003, Netflix succeeded in crossing 1 million subscribers and recorded its first annual profit. But during these days, Netflix has faced an immense competition from some of the industry giants. One of them was the well-known retail brand Wal Mart who in the year 2002 announced its entry into the online movie subscription services.

Wal Mart offered its service at $1 less than the Netflix, but it lacks in distribution service as it has one only one centralized distribution centre against ten leased by Netflix. Thus, unlike Netflix, Wal Mart failed to provide its customers with quicker delivery and forced to leave the market transferring its subscribers to Netflix.

Another competitor which came up with even a bigger challenge for Netflix was Blockbuster. It was fiercer since Blockbuster had a stronger brand image, a retail network of about 5500 stores across the country, and an extensive catalogue of movie titles. Once launched, it integrated with   it in-store rentals, giving an ease to customer to return the movie through mail or store. However, even after having an edge over Netflix in all these aspects, it failed to attract more customer than Netflix.

Amazon's announcement to enter into the UK market in online movie subscription was yet another threat in the row faced by Netflix. Amazon had already made its mark in the online retailing and logistics and delivery system, and this acted as a threat to Netflix. Thus, Netflix postponed its decision to enter UK and concentrated all its efforts to expand into US. This competition even resulted in the reduction in the monthly subscription fee charged by Netflix. However, this move was the perfect decision made by the company during that situation.

The challenges did not end here, the biggest of all include the change in technological standards of the customers. The DVD format was getting obsoleted in faster rate and was being replaced by instant viewing over the internet. While Hastings has recognized the threat, he tackled the situation smartly by justifying the name of the company which include NET symbolizing the use of internet for streaming movies. Meanwhile, Hastings strategized his next move where he entered into the licensing agreements with the studios that allows subscribers to download the limited selection of movie titles over the internet with no additional cost (other than the subscription fees). In addition, Netflix partnered with few of the hardware companies like LG, Samsung, Microsoft (Xbox), Sony (play station), etc. allowing users to watch downloaded movies directly on their television. Some of the factors which helped the company in dealing with the challenge is lack of broadband connections and subscriber base who still prefer DVD formats.

An Adult Culture- A new HRM Perspective:

Its not just prevailing over its competitors that made the Netflix standalone in the crowd, but the culture of freedom and responsibility Reed Hastings inculcated in the organization. He called it as an 'Adult Culture' which is characterized by hard work, initiatives, creativity, and accountability. It means company expect its employee to work hard, take a step ahead and show their creativity, take initiatives whenever required, take ownership of their own work, and putting the company's interest first. Adult like behavior is talking openly about issues with your boss, your colleagues, and your subordinates. And for this purpose, company too has taken an initiative by minimizing the rules and bureaucracy. In line with this culture, company prefers hiring those people who can handle the work of two or more people. In other words, Netflix only hires those people who are outstanding as these people saves cost and work more. And thus, company not only make efforts to attract these candidates but to retain them at any cost. Some of the highlights of Adult Culture at Netflix has been discussed in succeeding topics.

Excelling @ Employment Practices:

While supporting its adult culture, Netflix has incorporated various HR practices. And these practices help the company in reserving its place in the competitive business environment.

i. **Vacation Policy**: Initially the company has standard paid-time-off policy, where employees were given 10 vacation days, 10 holidays, and a few sick leaves. But eventually   the company has realized the need for an informal system rather than a formal one. Salaried employees were told to take leaves as per their requirement on the basis of mutual understanding. But while doing so, employees were expected to behave rationally, such that they should not take leaves when their presence is utmost important or could affect the work.

ii. **Travel Policy**: Again, when it comes to travel for official work Netflix opted for an in formalized system wherein employees were asked to behave frugally. Unlike other companies who appoint travel agents to do the bookings, employees at Netflix do it by themselves considering it as their own company. They saved money by letting employees book their own trips online.

iii. **Compensation**: The compensation plan at Netflix is unique and offers a compensation mix to its employees. Compensation offered to the employee is a mixture of cash and stock option. They have an option to invest some part of their salary in company stock under its Employee Stock Purchase Plan (ESPP), that too as per their discretion. As a part of perquisites, company is offering its employees with health, dental, vision, and life insurance. With regards to the vacation, company never restricts it employees unless it affects the company's performance. In a way, employees can avail unlimited vacation at the right time without hampering company's performance. Considering all these factors the company has devised a unique compensation system, which began to take shape in 2003 and was fully formed by 2006. The key components of this system were as follows:

- **Compensation Mix**: Employees were given an option to choose and allocate their total compensation between base salary and option to invest in stock option, at the end of each calendar year. However, the company retain the power to lower the proportion of compensation delivered in stock option. At the end of the year, employees could change their allocation for the subsequent year.However, changes to the allocation during the course of the year were not allowed.

- **Pricing**: Option grants were made monthly, with one-twelfth of the annual allocation granted and priced on the first trading day of each month. For example, an employee electing to receive $24,000 of the total salary in stock options would receive a monthly stock allocation of $2,000.

  The number of shares underlying each monthly allocation was calculated using the formula:

  *Number of shares = monthly allocation/(stock price on grant date*25 percent)*

- **Vesting**: Employees were allowed to exercise the grants as and when they are allotted, thus no vesting restriction were attached with the stock options. Restricted vesting limits an employee to receive the full value of the stocks until the vesting period completes. At Netflix, since the company believes in high performance they prefer not to put any kind of vesting restriction (which they called as golden handcuffs), as forcing an employee to stay might affect their performance. And Netflix, incent employees to perform and not to stay back forcefully.

- **Termination**: Upon the termination of employees, whether voluntary or involuntary, Netflix provide its employees to hold the unexercised options for the remainder of 10-year term. It is based on the grounds that these stocks are in exchange of the salary forgo by an employee during his term in the company, thus have all the right to exercise it.

- **Cash Bonuses**: Though the company provides no cash bonuses, it compensates the employee in that way which reflects the combination of base salary and bonuses. The company believed that a practice of no cash bonuses was consistent with its high-performance culture and willingness to terminate underperforming employees.

iv. **Dream Team Dynamics**: At Netflix the dynamics of team formation is different from its counterparts. It focuses not on an ideal team but what a team needs to accomplish over a period of time and how they can bring a difference in their present work. And once they are done with their work, then they analyse how well their team matched with required skills sets. Company deals with their employees with utmost honesty by communicating if any kind of mismatches between the present skill sets and the required skills sets, and expect them to take it like an adult. Thus, the team dynamics didn't measure them on whether they were excellent coaches or mentors or got their paperwork done on time. Great teams accomplish great work, and recruiting the right team was the top priority.

Netflix's core philosophy is *People Over Process*. Their version of the great workplace is not comprised of sushi lunches, great gyms, fancy offices, or frequent parties. But, the great workplace is a dream team in pursuit of ambitious common goals, for which they spend heavily. A dream team is something where employees learn the most, perform their best work, improve the fastest, and have the most fun. The company have developed a 'keeper test' for each of their employee. The test judges the managers on the basis of how much efforts they are putting in to keep or retain an employee (in a dream team), failing which they are prompted for severance package.

v. **Performance Appraisal and Management**: Unlike most companies, where an average performer gets an average rise in the compensation, at Netflix they get severance package. And that is the reason involuntary turnover in the company is almost double the voluntary turnover. The company has instituted an informal 360-degree face to face reviews wherein People were asked to identify things that colleagues should stop, start, or continue. While appraising and managing the performance of the employees, Netflix considers the recent market trends and changes in the jobs and responsibilities (not on the basis of merit or cost of living).

vi. **Retention**: As discussed, Netflix believes in hiring only the outstanding candidates and once hired it make all possible measures to retain that talent. The company's philosophy was clear in this respect, it offers top-of-the market compensation to its employees and pay them more than anyone could do. While retaining its employees, Netflix pay them as much as a replacement would cost. Thus, company pays them with the highest packages which a competitor would have paid elsewhere.

vii. **Culture of Freedom and Responsibility**: At Netflix, employees are provided with utmost freedom to act and take the important decision in the company's interest. Some of these initiative by the company in this respect are as follows:

- **Systematic sharing** of company-related document at internal level, where employees have access to various company related information

- **No control** over signing of any contract, until it is well thought and based on good judgment

- Encouragement to the new parents to take leaves as and when they feel appropriate to take care of their baby and themselves

- No formal policy related to dressing at work place

Some of the exceptions to this culture are:

- o No compromise with ethical and safety issues

- o Zero tolerance to workplace harassment and trading on insider information

Thus, we can summarize the Culture at Netflix into five major points:

- Encourage independent decision-making by employees

- Share information openly, broadly and deliberately

- Are extraordinarily candid with each other

- Keep only highly effective people

- Avoid rules

Conclusions:

Corporate culture is nothing but ideology behind an organization— which includes its common principles, ideals, standards, and people it is something that is very intangible which serves as a pillar of reinforcement for corporate progress and achievement Yet many organizations fail to act sensibly to create their own unique identity—their own culture. Nonetheless, organizations such as NETFLIX have created an ass in building up a high-performance corporate culture by their innovative activities (let's not name them policies) they believe in giving their workers absolute independence and autonomy to operate with limited formalization. It thrives in creating a full adult culture and summarizes its work in one clear line 'Act in the best interest of NETFLIX. Netflix was founded when its CEO Reed Hastings saw an chance to solve a basic math question in DVD business. And from there the concept evolved and became a $61.6 billion net worth business. The organization is involved in providing broadband content to its clients, downloading videos and TV shows via the Broadband, and sending DVDs via fax.The jobs and selection requirements, fair pay systems, a straight-forward solution to non-performers, lucrative severance payments, the possibility of selecting a balance of wage and equity, etc. are some of the specific fields addressed in the event. The business was not possible to remain tall in view of rivals such as Amazon, Blockbuster, etc. The final area addressed by the event is how successfully NETFLIX has embraced the transition taking place in the external climate. This involves embracing and introducing technical improvements seamlessly while keeping a compromise between consumer desires and demands.

Case questions:

1. Which is the focus strengths of Netflix focused on the current operating model?

2. Why are Netflix's vital practices and services impacted by the change from DVD rentals to video distribution and original content?

3. Which are the current expected results of Netflix focused on the latest distribution goal model?

20. What Happened to Old McDonalds?

A Case Study in Brand Management & Strategy Management

Learning Objectives:

1. To understand the capital structure pattern of Mc Donald's restaurants; American capitalism's greatest success stories, reputable brand image and a memorable history.

2. To understand the main objectives of McDonald's for adapting to the changing demand of its customers and the customers' perception for McDonald's food quality.

3. To understand the Maintenance of the traditional efficiency of fast food restaurant and provide comfortable environment to customers and changing market demand and standards.

4. To study the McDonald's Branding Strategy, Marketing Strategy, Market analysis and Market Share Model.

5. To understand the McDonald's Brand crisis, reputation, PR& crisis management, Market segmentation, product development, market development &the main reason/ reasons for a big corporation to fall.

Synopsis:

McDonald's, the seemingly invincible fast food giant and stalwart of American business, has been an ironclad money-making machine for decades now. Sure, they've had their issues with bad press concerning the negative health effects of their food, but otherwise the company is as sure to post profits quarter after quarter as anyone. At least that's been true until recently, as it appears that McDonald's has hit a bit of a snag. Starting out with just one burger stall in 1948, the fast-food chain's emphasis on quick service and a standardized menu has helped it to grow to more than 35,000 outlets across the world. It has been profitable: after a wobbly period in the early 2000s, the firm's share price went from $12 in 2003 to more than

$100 at the end of 2011. But now McDonald's has lost its sizzle. Global sales have been declining at least since last July. When the company announces its annual results on January 23rd, analysts think it will reveal its first full-year fall in like-for-like revenues since 2002.

What's Gone Wrong?

Some of McDonald's problems stem from operational mishaps across the world. In particular, its business in Asia—where it makes nearly a quarter of its global revenues—has been hit by several health scares. Sales in China fell sharply after one of its suppliers was discovered last July to be using expired and contaminated chicken and beef. More recently, several Japanese customers have reported finding bits of plastic and even a tooth in their food. Geopolitics has not helped. Last year some Russian outlets were temporarily closed by food inspectors, seemingly, in retaliation for American and European sanctions against Russia over its military intervention in Ukraine.

Some politicians in Russia have even called for the chain to be thrown out of the country completely. But McDonald's also has problems at home. It faces competition from other fast- food chains such as Burger King, which has been gaining market share with a simpler and cheaper version of the McDonald's menu. And it is being squeezed by more up market "fast-casual" restaurants such as Shake Shack andChipotle Mexican Grill, which are rapidly growing. They have been luring customers—particularly younger ones— away from

McDonald's chicken nuggets and chips by offering slightly better quality food, a high level of customization (such as the option to choose the ingredients in a burrito or burger) and some table service. McDonald's seems to have two options: to emulate the likes of Burger King and go back to basics, or to spruce itself up to compete with the likes of Shake Shack. The chain seems to be trying to do both. It now has two new formats, one offering a simpler menu, and another called "Create your taste", letting customers customize their burgers. Similarly, it has opened "Mc Cafés" in several countries. In France, one of the few parts of the world where McDonald's sales are still rising, these offer macaroons, tea and coffee in china cups and saucers, as well as some limited waitress service. It hasn't always gone smoothly: some of the restaurants in Paris were forced to put signs on the bins saying "please do not throw away the crockery". As McDonald's tries to reinvent itself, it may find that disposing of its traditional image will prove much harder. In a brand-new McDonald's outlet near its headquarters in Oak Brook, Illinois, customers do not have to queue at the counter. They can go to a touch screen and build their own burger by choosing a bun, toppings and sauces from a list of more than 20 "premium" ingredients, including grilled mushrooms, guacamole and caramelized onions. Then they sit down, waiting an average of seven minutes until a server brings their burgers to their table. The company is planning to roll out its "Create Your Taste" burgers in up to 2,000 restaurants - it is not saying where - by late 2015, and possibly in more places if they do well.

McDonald's is also trying to engage with customers on social media and is working on a smart phone app, as well as testing mobile-payment systems such as Apple Pay, Soft card and Google Wallet. All this is part of the "Experience of the Future", a plan to revive the flagging popularity of McDonald's, especially among younger consumers. "We are taking decisive action to change fundamentally the way we approach our business," says Heidi Barker, a spokeswoman.

After a successful run which lifted the firm's share price from $12 in 2003 to more than $100 at the end of 2011, McDonald's had a tricky 2013 and a much harder time last year. When it announces its annual results on January 23rd, some analysts fear it will reveal a drop in global "like-for-like" sales (ie, after stripping out the effect of opening new outlets) for the whole of 2014 - the first such fall since 2002.

In the past year, Don Thompson, the firm's relatively new boss, has had to fight fires around the world, some of them beyond his control.

Sales in China fell sharply after a local meat supplier was found guilty of using expired, contaminated chicken and beef. The biggest problem has been in America—by far McDonald's largest market, where it has 14,200 of its 35,000 mostly franchised restaurants. In November its American like-for-like sales were down 4.6% a year earlier.

It had weathered the 2008-09 recession and its aftermath by attracting cash-strapped consumers looking for a cheap bite. But more recently, it has been squeezed by competition from Burger King, revitalized under the management of a private-equity firm, from other fast-food joints such as Subway and Starbucks, and from the growing popularity of slightly more up market "fast casual" outlets. In response, McDonald's has expanded its menu with all manner of wraps, salads and so on. Its American menu now has almost 200 items. This strains kitchen staff and annoys franchisees, who often have to buy new equipment. It may also deter customers. "McDonald's stands for value, consistency and convenience," says Darren Tristano at Technomic, a restaurant-industry consultant, and it needs to stay true to this. Most diners want a Big Mac or a Quarter Pounder at a good price, served quickly. And, as company executives now acknowledge, its strategy of reeling in diners with a "Dollar Menu" then trying to tempt them with pricier dishes is not working.

McDonald's says it has got the message and is experimenting in some parts of America with a simpler menu: one type of Quarter Pounder with cheese rather than four; one Snack Wrap rather than three; and so on. However, this seems to run contrary to the build-your-burger strategy it is trying elsewhere, which expands the number of choices. That in turn is McDonald's response to the popularity of "better burger" chains, such as Shake Shack, which has just filed for stock market floatation. Some analysts think that McDonald's should stop trying to replicate all its rivals' offerings and go back to basics, offering a limited range of dishes at low prices, served freshly and quickly.

Sara, Senator of Sanford, C. Bernstein, a research outfit, notes that Burger King, having struggled against its big rival for years, has begun to do better with a simpler and cheaper version of the McDonald's menu. For the third quarter of 2014 Burger King reported a like-for-like sales increase of 3.6% in America and Canada compared with a decrease by 3.3% of comparable sales at McDonald's. That said, sales at an average McDonald's in America are still roughly double those of an average Burger King. So the case for going back to basics remains unproven.

So far, McDonald's looks as if it is undergoing a milder version of its last crisis, in 2002-03. Then, an over-rapid expansion had damaged its reputation for good service, its menu had become bloated and customers were drifting to rivals claiming to offer healthier food. Now, once again, "McDonald's has a huge image problem in America," says John Gordon, a restaurant expert at the Pacific Management Consulting Group. This is in part because of its use of frozen "factory food" packed with preservatives. In 2013 a story about a 14-year-old McDonald's burger that had not rotted received huge coverage. Even Mike Andres, the new boss of the company's American operations, recently asked bemused investors: "Why do we need to have preservatives in our food?" and then answered himself: "We probably don't". McDonald's doesn't seem to be cool any more, especially among youngsters. Parents say their teenage children have been put off after seeing "Super-Size Me", a documentary about surviving only on McDonald's food; and "Food, Inc", another about the corporatization of the food industry; and by reading "Fast Food Nation: The Dark Side of the All-American Meal". It is hard to imagine the new McDonald's initiatives getting the reaction Shake Shack got when it opened its first outlet in downtown Chicago in November: for the first two weeks it had long queues of people waiting outside in the freezing cold. A lot of the negative PR that McDonald's gets is the flipside of being the world's biggest and most famous fast- food chain. This has made it the whipping-boy of food activists, labor activists, animal-rights campaigners and those who simply dislike all things American.

In America it has been the focus of a campaign for fast-food workers and others to get a minimum salary of $15 an hour and the right to unionize. Last month the National Labor Relations Board, a federal agency, released details of 13 complaints against McDonald's and many of its franchisees for violating employees' rights to campaign for better pay and working conditions. The alleged violations relate to threats, surveillance, discrimination, reduced hours and even sackings of workers who supported the protests. McDonald's contests these charges, while arguing that it is not responsible for its franchisees' labor practices.

Not all the criticism McDonald's gets may be merited—or at least it should be shared more fairly with its peers. However, the company's troubles have begun to attract the attention of activist shareholders, who may prove somewhat harder to brush aside than labor or food activists. In November Jana Partners, an activist fund, took a stake in the firm. Then in December its shares jumped, on rumors that one of the most prominent and determined activists, Bill Ackman, intended to buy a stake and press for a shake-up. McDonald's says it welcomes all investors and is focused on maximizing value for its shareholders. Even so, Mr Thompson's new strategy needs to deliver results quickly. MrAckman's Pershing Square Capital has done well out of its 11% stake in Burger King, because the chain's main shareholder, 3G Capital, has pushed through a drastic cost- cutting program and a merger with Tim Hortons, a Canadian restaurant group. "If McDonald's were run like Burger King, the stock would go up a lot," MrAckman mused recently.

It looks like Mr Thompson may soon have to fight on another front. The documental that helped this crisis go horribly wrong McDonalds is a famous fast food chain around the world. There it has nearly 32,00 local restaurants in more than 100 countries. The first thing anyone will remember after listening to McDonalds is 'BIG Mac'. In 2004 a director called Morgan Spurlock made a documentary movie on McDonalds. This movie was all about how McDonald's foods affect human body and health condition. He ate McDonalds for 1 month for breakfast, lunch and dinner. After 1 month he gained weight, his blood pressure was high and so on. He increased 5% of his body mass during 1 week of the month. This movie effected McDonald's reputation very negatively. It decreased the sale of McDonalds by 42 million dollar in the USA. Two overweight girls from New York tried to sue McDonalds for their health condition. After this movie McDonalds tried to change their menu plan. They added healthy and organic foods in their menu. They introduced salads, milk shakes, grilled burgers and so on. They also changed the environment of their restaurants they painted their restaurants in to bright colors to attract the customers. They started gifting toys with the kid's meal.

They added less oily food in their menu such as snack wrap. McDonalds also stopped selling super-size portion in most of their restaurants. They arranged a place for children to play. They also arranged games competitions for school children. This is to show that they are supportive towards the physical activities for the customers.

These are some of the ways McDonalds tried to overcome the negative effects of the Super -size movie on their reputation. They were also successful in making their reputation better as their sales increased every month. In 2008 the global sales of McDonalds increased by 6.9%.Their total revenue in 2008 was 23.5 billion dollar cash returned to the stakeholders were 5.8 billion dollars in 2008.

To sum up it can be said that McDonalds was badly affected by the movie 'Super-Size Me'. That movie represented McDonalds as an unhealthy fast food chain. But McDonalds effectively carried out damage control exercise by introducing healthy and organic food along with burgers and chips.

McCafe's expansion over the last few years McDonald's has been giving a lot of attention to the expansion of its coffee portfolio, by increasing the presence of McCafe in McDonald's stores. With more than 11,000 stores in the U.S. having McCafe coffee stations, the U.S. customers are already well aware of the brand. However, its popularity is not as widespread as that of Starbucks' coffee or Dunkin? Donuts coffee. The reason behind this disparity is the perception of McDonald?s among U.S. customers. McDonalds has been considered as a typical fast food chain, which serves on-the-go fast food items and hamburgers, whereas chains, such as Starbucks, are premium coffee restaurants, with their main focus on coffee service. However, McDonald's has been trying to change this common perception by expanding the number of McCafe coffee stations, as well as by introducing McCafe to retail stores.

In August 2014, McDonald's and Kraft Foods Group announced a deal to expand the manufacture, marketing, and distribution of McDonald's McCafe brand in the U.S., with effect from early 2015. Shortly after this deal, Kraft Foods entered into a multi-year licensing, manufacturing, and distribution deal with the Vermont based K-Cups maker, Keurig Green Mountain.

After its plans for introducing McCafe in the U.S., the company decided to expand the reach of its coffee product in Canada, which is its fifth largest market in terms of number of restaurants. In such a market, where almost 95% markets dominated by well established brands, McCafe might find it difficult to penetrate the Canadian market effectively. Customers will need a strong reason to shift their coffee preferences from the likes of Starbucks and Tim Hortons to McCafe. This might create problems for McDonald's to generate expected sales in the initial years. However, one of the most prominent reasons for people to shift to McDonald's coffee is that McCafe is slightly cheaper compared to Starbucks' coffee. McCafe's success in Canada might provide a huge boost to the company to expand its McCafe portfolio in its other major markets in Europe and Asia.

McDonalds plans to make another effort to increase its sales in the coming year. The corporation rolls out its plan to reverse the free fall. In addition to removing human antibiotics from its chicken and introducing a bigger, third of a pound burger to its menu, the company's current CEO says it will focus on making food of better quality overall. Despite what they want you to believe, McDonald's was never about the food. There was always better food elsewhere. McDonald's was about the kids, and the parents deserving a "break". Now that parents don't have to bring the kids to McDonald's to get the latest Happy Meal toy, I see McDonald's suffering the same fate as the Mc DLT and the fried Hot Apple Pie.

Outcome:

The outcome is that customers not only require the product to fulfill their needs but the value to be derived from the product as well as the level of satisfaction gained. Thus it can be said that brands need to work upon creating value and satisfaction to win the customers as it happened with McDonalds in India-segmented the market, targeted and positioned. Brands need to study the markets thoroughly so as to gain the knowledge about the changing tastes and preferences of the customers and to avoid any decline in the product life cycle. Strategies should be framed in a way that the products occupy the place in the minds of the customers. It is not the brand which is old but the strategies which are renewed. Brands which come up with a bang and make a revival are assumed to occupy the market more efficiently.

Conclusion:

Each product has a brand; and every brand has a core value. This core value is shaped by the customers a company attracts. This core value should be unique, different from other products. Once a company understands its core value, it helps the company to create an impressive brand. McDonald's brand was clear before the rice dishes were introduced: an American style fast food restaurant. When people go to McDonald's, they expect to enjoy all sorts of high-calorie, greasy, yet so delicious American fast food. This type of food is exactly what people want from McDonald's. The connection between the food it serves and McDonald's brand is strong.

When localizing a product, companies must make sure their new products consistently resonate with their original brand. It is true that some localization will make the product more acceptable for a local culture. McDonald's failure provides a valuable lesson: when a localized product is disconnected from the company's own brand and core value, the customers will be lost, the company is likely to suffer, and the product is all likelihood will fail. Therefore, although innovation is important, reliable market research is also key, some ideas that may work later don't necessarily fit the current market trend as intended.

Case Questions:

1.1. Do you think McDonald´s will recover after all the PR scandals and quality issues?

1.2. Have McDonald´s forgotten their recipe of success? What do you think is the main issue in McDonald´s fall?

1.3. Do you think the documentary "Super-Size Me" was a major reason for this crisis?

21. 'Managing Business with respect'

A Case Study on ITC

Learning Objectives:

1. To Identify, evaluate, and develop marketing strategies of ITC in India.

2. To Evaluate the sustainability of competitive advantages

3. To detect the cross industry variation in the strategic orientation.

4. To assess the focus of selected organizations on individual variants of strategic management viz. strategic intent, strategic formulation, strategic implementation and strategic control.

5. To detect the loopholes in the strategic orientation of the ITC which might have retarded their operating efficiency.

6. To give some practicable suggestions to the selected large organizations so that these may make necessary changes in their strategic outlook for competitive advantage.

Synopsis:

The ITC company was incorporated in 1910. Much has changed in these 100 years. ITC itself has metamorphosed in many ways, the least of which is the multiple changes in nomenclature. What began and stayed for long as only a cigarette maker has turned into a conglomerate offering a dashboard of products and services, ranging from hospitality to toiletry to apparel to food. Of course, cigarettes remain a big but gradually shrinking part of its overall business.

ITC had a market cap of over Rs 100,000 crore and ended 2008-09 with a turnover of Rs 15,582 crore. It employs over 26,000 people at more than 60 locations across India and has 338,000 shareholders.

It is but one of scores of India's centurion companies. Among others, Andrew Yule is alive and kicking even at 130 years of age. Then there are Allahabad Bank, Walchandnagar Industries, Tata Steel, Bank of Baroda, Indian Bank, Alembic, Corporation Bank, Canara Bank, Bank of India, Shalimar Paints, Indian Hotels, Spencer& Company, Century Textiles, Punjab National Bank and Bombay Dyeing. Many companies were originally British and became Indian through the fifties, sixties and seventies. There are many that assumed Indian names after take overs by home-grown business houses.

Originally incorporated as Imperial Tobacco Company of India, ITC too has undergone a few name changes. As its ownership became largely Indian, it became India Tobacco Company in 1970. Then, keeping in fashion of the day, it abbreviated itself to ITC in 1974. That was in recognition of its changing business portfolio, which by then included hotels. Later it was to add information technology, packaging, paperboards & specialty papers, agricultural business, foods, lifestyle retailing, education & stationery products, personal care and clothing.

Very few Indian companies have reinvented themselves as ITC has. Realizing long ago that cigarette cannot be its bread and butter for long, given the rising campaign against smoking, the company first moved into hotels and then into the FMCG business – both have brought handsome rewards. Even in organizational matters, it has brought about vast changes. For example, its divisional CEOs run their businesses almost independently; yet there's a high level of synergy across those businesses.

Much of the change has come about under the stewardship of chairman YC Deveshwar, who has adopted a three-pronged strategy to continue growth in the years to come. As ITC officials say the strategy is to "emerge as a sustainable company with national priorities and further Indians capital and resources".

ITC and Its Business Ideology:

"The company will increasingly focus on volume-based businesses and areas with the highest scope for direct interface with customers. It will strive to turn as many brands as possible into market leaders, officials in the know say.

"It is the right move at the right time, the company could survive and grow for so long simply because of its professional management and thrust on training and retraining of employees. One of every seven employees is sent for extensive training and, if need be, re-training. As the company reinvents itself, its employees are also re-trained."

The company's transformation started in 1968 was not easy or smooth. "ITC's overseas shareholders were only interested in the tobacco business. ITC had to convince them so that they stay invested in the company. Dealing with the government on various approval-related issues was not easy either.

The former vice-chairman and director of corporate strategies of ITC said the recent strategies had been working wonders for the company "We have all along stayed away from very high tech areas. Over the years, the company has concentrated on -- and should continue to concentrate on -- socially relevant areas, where there are volumes and higher customer contacts like hotel, paper, etc., and areas where the company can leverage its proverbial distribution network.

For six decades after its inception, the focus was solely on cigarettes and leaf tobacco business; the seventies saw the beginnings of a corporate transformation. According to its website, the company's diversified status originates from its corporate strategy aimed at creating multiple drivers of growth anchored on distribution reach, brand-building, effective supply chain management and service skills in the hotel business.

The packaging & printing business was set up in 1925 as a strategic backward integration for the cigarettes business. The hotel business was started in 1975 with the acquisition of a hotel in Chennai. The property was later rechristened ITC- Welcome Group Today, the company has over 100 owned and managed properties spread across India.

In 1979 ITC entered the paperboards business by promoting ITC Bhadrachalam Paperboards, which today has become the market leader in India. Bhadrachalam Paper boards amalgamated with ITC in March 2002 and became a division. In November the same year this division merged with the company's Tribeni Tissues division to form the paperboards & specialty papers division.

In 1990, leveraging its sourcing competency, ITC set up the agricultural business division for export of commodities. The division is today one of India's largest exporters. Ten years later, it started what was then unique and by now widely acknowledged e-copal initiative with soya farmers in Madhya Pradesh. Now it extends to 10 states covering over four million farmers.

Also in 2000 ITC forayed into the greeting, gifting and stationery product business with the launch of the 'Expressions' range of greeting cards. A line of premium range of notebooks under the Paper Kraft brand was launched in 2002. A year later, it launched the 'Classmate' brand of notebooks to reach a wider body of students. It is now India's biggest notebook brand which includes school bags. Between 2007 and 2009, it launched children's books, geometry boxes, pens and pencils too. Life style retailing was embraced in 2000 with the Wills Sport range for men and women. Within two years it widened its portfolio with the men's wear brand, John Players. The information technology business was turned into a wholly owned subsidiary, ITC InfoTech India, in 2000.

ITC stepped into the foods business in 2001 with a range of ready-to-eat Indian gourmet dishes under the Kitchens of India brand. Then came the confectionery and staples segments with Mint-O and Candyman and Aashirvaad atta (wheat flour). Sun feast biscuits followed quickly.

The next move was a logical extension of the food business. Bingo, the snack brand, came in 2007. In eight years, the foods business has grown significantly, with over 200 differentiated products under six distinctive brands. Among other products launched in the past eight years are safety matches and agarbattis, the latter in partnership with the cottage sector. In Toiletry, ITC's Fiama Di Wills, a premium range of shampoos, shower gels and soaps came in quick succession in the last four months of 2007. Around the same time, the mass-market and shampoos were introduced. The higher-end Vivel de Wills and Vivel range of soaps and shampoos came in 2008.

ITC has made a successful transition from being a cigarettes company to a consumer goods seller in the past two years. Its consumer goods portfolio, today, includes soaps, shampoos, biscuits, and salty snacks among others.

ITC Distribution strategy:

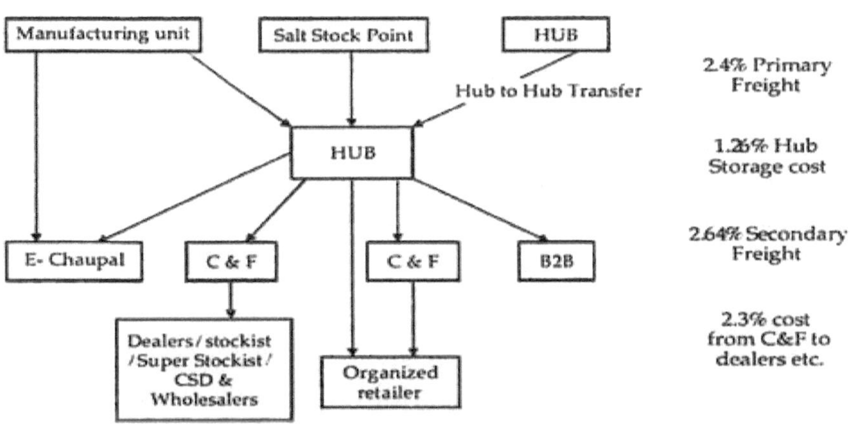

These are all extremely competitive consumer categories with well entrenched multinational as well as domestic players such as Hindustan Unilever, Procter & Gamble, Dabur and Marico. With the right product and marketing mix, ITC has not only managed to create a space for itself in this overly-crowded consumer segment but has built a strong brand recall as well among its target consumers. In 2009, the company launched variants of its popular salty snack brand Bingo! Chips. The launch was well supported by a brilliant advertising campaign that won consumers' attention as well immense creative applaud.

Starting with the first of the Bingo! commercials, which showed scientists falling over themselves in selecting the best of three identical triangles, aka Bingo! Mad Angles, the ads have continued with their irreverent and humorous messaging. The latest are its Bingo! Red Chilli Bijli and Bingo! International Cream and Onion Potato variants, which have helped the brand cater to every palate. At a time when most rivals were reeling under tremendous cost pressures and depressed consumer demand, the company has registered impressive results on the back of a good product mix, smart sourcing of raw materials, and several cost management steps. Its non-cigarette FMCG segment continued to improve on profitability while revenues from the sector grew 14% in the July-September 2009 quarter. Investments in brand building in the FMCG segment have also brought in handsome results. Higher taxes notwithstanding, cigarette sales grew impressively and so did the rural agri-business.

The company says it's the focus on innovation and specific consumer needs that have enabled its business to deliver superior value. A well-crafted portfolio of brands with a good blend of contemporary packaging and marketing communication, is the other secret to tits success.

Water-positive and carbon-positive, India's largest cigarette maker ITC is known almost as much for its other activities now.

That has earned it new respect, and fueled growth at a time when the core business is facing limitations.

That is what ITC has accomplished through decades of focus on sustainability and corporate social responsibility. In fact, it has achieved the near-impossible of diverting attention away from its core business of tobacco, which pooled in 48 per cent of its turnover some years ago.

"For six years in a row, ITC has been a water-positive company, and for three consecutive years to date, we have sustained our carbon-positive status, notwithstanding the large growth in our business. Today, we have three times more fresh water harvesting potential than what we consume and sequester almost twice the amount of carbon we emit. This year, we have also achieved the 100 per cent benchmark in recycling solid waste in several of our operations. This makes us the only company in the world, of our size and diversity, to have achieved these three milestones," said Yogi C Deveshwar, the company's Ex chairman.

The journey to these milestones has been paved by several gallons of midnight oil burnt by ITC executives to resolve tricky issues. In hotels, for instance, the challenge lies in disposal of food from the kitchen, and of the old linen and towels that pile up in the store. The solutions are innovative — tying up with piggeries to utilize food fit for animal consumption and converting the rest into compost to be used as manure. The linen and towels are given away to orphanages. Leftover ghee and oil in the kitchens is transported to a soap factory to be used as raw material.

The challenges were the biggest for ITC's Bhadrachalam paperboard plant, which generates enormous solid waste. The fly ash generated from the boilers in the mill is used to make bricks. And to demonstrate that the fly ash bricks are as durable as their more conventional counterparts, they have been used by the company to build its own staff colony.

Agriculture Entrance of ITC: E –Choupal:

Today, the company has 6,500 e-Chou pals (internet-driven knowledge kiosks that give farmers information and services for all aspects of farming) covering 40,000 villages and over 4 million farmers, and a social forestry initiative that has greened over 80,000 hectares and created 35 million man days of employment.

For long a force in the hospitality sector (Maurya), it has become a major player in the areas of apparel (Wills Lifestyle) and foods (Sunfeast, Ashirvaad, Kitchens of India). When it comes to public perception, these have become as prominent, if not more, than ITC's cigarette brands, which do not make for a happy discussion at public forums and whose advertising avenues are restricted by law. Still, the fact is that the company pays its bills and its shareholders with tobacco money. Many of the new businesses, funded by the earnings from tobacco, have yet to stop being a drain on the resources

That raises the uncomfortable question: does this whole thing amount so far too little more than a corporate social responsibility, or CSR, initiative to make people stop linking ITC to tobacco? Or is there deep strategic thinking behind it? The answer is complexity's diversification thrust started early with forays into paper manufacturing, deep-sea fishing and hospitality ventures. But it's only recently, after more than 35 years of sustained efforts — that ITC has come to be seen as an entity that creates value for both stakeholders and society at large. With the launch of e-Chou pals in 2000, ITC took a bold step towards aligning its business goals with the empowerment of farmers and help farmers get real-time access to farming knowledge, weather information, and transparent price comparisons.

When ITC diversified into packaged foods with the launch of the 'Kitchens of India' brand in 2001, e-Chou pal provided the confidence of a bolstered supply chain. "The cost-efficient sourcing and identity-preservation of raw agri-materials such as wheat and potato have been the key factors for the rapid success of ITC's branded foods business.

Potatoes form a large part of its snack foods business, while wheat supply is critical for packaged wheat flour. No less than a million tons of wheat is sourced through e-Choupals to replenish its thriving wheat flour brand, Aashirvaad. Launched in 2002, Aashirvaad has already left its closest rival, Hindustan Unilever's Annapurna, behind and appropriated over 50 per cent of the market for itself. The subtle, unadvertised regional customization in the atta's composition has worked to make it the preferred brand. The ease with which ITC can interact with farmers, thanks to e-Choupal's backward integration, has enabled the company to get the right crop mix of wheat varieties to cater to different regional palates. The last but vital task of mixing and churning the wheat flour, so it gets cooked the way home-makers want, is ensured by the company's legacy of blending tobacco. The wheat supply has not only helped Aashirvad lord it over the branded atta market, it has also provided the dough for its line of biscuits, whose sales, according to market estimates, scaled Rs 700 crore in 2006, when market leader Britannia's turnover was Rs 1,500 crore.

E-Choupals have armed ITC with a rural retail network that has organized retailers queuing up to tap it. For every 40 e-Choupals, ITC has one Choupal Sagar a physical marketing hub where farmers can get hands-on training, hire a tractor, or just shop for FMCGs and durables. The next couple of years witnessed ITC managing the back-end operations logistics, warehousing and stores of the likes of Food Bazaar and India Bulls Marts, leveraging its ChoupalSagar experience.

Much before e-Choupal captured the popular imagination, ITC was working with marginal farmers as part of its paperboards business. The association, however, was borne as much out of necessity as intent. Bhadrachalam Paperboards Ltd, set up in Andhra Pradesh in 1975, which later merged with the parent company in 2001 to form ITC's paperboards and specialty papers division, ventured into farm forestry in the early 1980s, when government regulations made it tough to source raw material from the forests located around the establishment.

The challenge lay in finding an alternative source of wood pulp that would not resort to imports and one that would be faster than the erstwhile seven years of plant maturing. The company hit upon a plan that would not only ensure a steady supply of raw materials but also provide year-around jobs to farmers. It tied up with small and marginal farmers of the region who would raise fast-growing plantations for the factory. The idea saw wastelands growing pulpwood plantations that yielded three times more pulp and supplied 90 per cent of the woody raw material that kept the huge Bhadrachalam machines rolling.

Today, with access to 80,000 hectares, ITC has become one of the first carbon-positive corporations of its size and complexity in the world. As many as 13,492 households in 406 villages are earning more than their seasonal farming wages. So successful has ITC's paperboards business been, the company claims, that it consumes just 20 per cent of the over 4,70,000 tons per annum of manufactured paper-boards it produces, with the rest meeting the demand of other companies. The business has clocked a profit of Rs 124 crore (an increase of 43 per cent year-on-year) supplying to other corporations and ITC's own businesses that involve packaging for its food, tobacco and personal care products.

For ITC, starting to do good for society couldn't have comeat a better time. Much of it coincided with the government's clamping down on tobacco products and anti-smoking legislation being passed. ITC ran the risk of being saddled with a primary business that could only gain stronger pejorative shades: cigarettes. The anti-tobacco lobby, often training its guns on the cigarette industry, was backed by the government when it amended the Cable TV Act in 1995, culminating in the ministry of information and broadcasting banning cigarette advertisements in 2000. Even surrogate advertising was banned in 2002.The company, of course, could still have done without advertisements, backed as it was with nearly a decade-old legacy and a distribution reach few Indian companies could boast of. But the clampdown has seeped into the government's taxation patterns as well, and ITC, like its peers, felt the heat.

With the mounting taxes — from excise duties to value-added tax — the company could not miss the negative vibes. It was only a matter of time before the rising tax burden eroded ITC's robust revenues from the Rs 6,635-crore cigarette business (FY08 estimates) for a capital employed of Rs 2314.64 crore (that powers all its new ventures). The ever-increasing tax levies have shrunk the cigarette market as well, with many downgrading to low-cost but more harmful tobacco options such as khaini and gutkha.

Paperboards and foods are perhaps the first two in a series of businesses to come supported by ITC's sustainability efforts. For example, the livestock development program a part of ITC's 'SunheraKal' project, which has started to supplement those families which are in the immediate catchment areas of their factories (in Munger, Bihar, for instance) may one day equip ITC with the resources for dairy farming.

ITC had not expanded into new businesses and stayed with just cigarettes, the top lines growth would have come much slower. There has been a paradigm shift in diversification under the leadership of Deveshwar. "With the accelerated growth, the new businesses, especially the non-cigarette FMCG portfolio, account for over 50 per cent of our turnover. It has been a strategic decision to grow through FMCG. most of the ITC FMCG divisions already have 8 to 10 per cent of the market, and lead in the Atta market. "Some of ITC's businesses have exhibited enviable speed, with the snacks brand 'Bingo' reportedly securing 11 per cent of the market within six months of its launch in 2007. ITC claims a market share of 40-45 per cent in the packaged food market and almost 12 per cent in snacks.

The company knows that in the long run, consumers, especially the business-to-business ones, will settle for an environmentally-conscious company. The business customers prefer the carbon-neutrality in ITC's packaging and paper businesses, which are produced through the elemental-chlorine-free technology that is kind on the environment. "When we talk to international customers such as Wal-Mart, they question us on sustainability, which has now become a qualifier: "The awareness of what the company does today is much higher than in our time. I think ITC is now respected even more." says a company executive

ITC has carefully reduced the presence of the cigarette business and focusing much more on its fresh ventures and achievements as a corporate citizen. A clever re-branding has taken the Wills brand's association much beyond cigarettes, so that the equity built over the decades because of ITC's dominance of the cigarette market is reaped by other products like apparel. While cigarettes generated Rs 961.41 crore in profits in the first quarter of 2009, the non-tobacco FMCG products eroded Rs 122.61 crore. The hotels, agri-business, and paperboards and packaging have registered year-on-year growth rates ranging from 33 to 43 per cent. The new business of readymade clothing retail, too, is making dents in ITC's profit.

But ITC's socially-relevant programs will come to its rescue to support the gestation of new businesses. ITC's exports continue to strengthen farmers, who are its key suppliers, the spread of ChoupalSagars has ensured that the company's FMCG products (except for the high-end) are within reach of the rural population. So there, a whole new yardstick now measures the work done in ITC's offices and in the outfields, compelling the rest of the world to take a whole new view

ITC forges in sustainable business models focused on rural India.

1. ITC schemes:

- e-choupal initiative is designed to enhance farm productivity and provide market linkages.

- Social forestry scheme has greened over 80,000 hectares.

- R&D projects have evolved high-yielding, site specific, disease-resistant clones.

- Comprehensive package of plantation management practices

- Watershed development projects benefit 33,311 farmers in 24 districts.

In an increasingly inter-connected world, stakeholders including investors and consumers have raised the bar of expectations from private sector in terms of their response to issues of ethics, transparency and sustainability concerns.

2. e-choupal

ITC's e-choupal initiative, designed to enhance farm productivity and provide market linkages and numbering 6,500, cover 40,000 villages and benefit over four million farmers.

3. Social forestry

The social forestry initiative of the company has greened over

80,000 hectares and created cumulative employment of 35 million man-days, besides providing a reliable source of wood pulp for the long-term competitiveness and sustainability of ITC's paper business.

4. Plantation management

Over 93 per cent of the company's Bhadrachalam mill's aggregate wood need in 2007-08 came from plantations initiated through the forestry project undertaken by tribal and marginal farmers. As the availability of wood, the prime source of fiber for the paper and paperboards remains a key challenge and concern for sustainability, the company's R&D initiatives have evolved high-yielding, disease-resistant clones and a comprehensive package of plantation management practices.

The sustainability report said the company is committed to green one lakh hectares in the next few years, which would far exceed its wood fiber requirement, foster livelihood chances for a very large number of people in tribal belts and further consolidate its position as a 'carbon positive' corporation.

5. Renewable energy

What is particularly noteworthy is that 96 per cent of the company's energy requirements are panned out internally with more than 24 per cent of energy generated from renewable resources.

The report also highlights that ITC has been a "water positive' firm and today the company generates three times more freshwater harvesting potential than it consumes and sequesters almost twice the amount of carbon its plants emit.

6. Recycling solid waste

In 2007-08, the company also compassed the 100 per cent

benchmark in recycling solid waste in several of its operations. Moreover, the company's watershed development projects now assist farmers in 24 districts, benefiting 33,311 farmers. A total of 2,178 water harvesting structures have been created, providing critical irrigation to 18,483 hectares of farmland.

Finally, ITC's 'Mission Sunehra Kal' encompassing its sustainable development initiatives would continue to provide thrust to identified triple interventions viz., natural resource management (wasteland, watershed and agriculture development), sustainable livelihoods comprising genetic improvement in livestock and economic empowerment of women and community development with focus on primary education, health and sanitation.

Social policy analysts contend that if corporate social responsibility (CSR) is taken by all big companies earnestly with a view to building public-private partnership for sustainable and inclusive growth, the simmering tensions and resistance to industrial development through setting up economic enclaves or big projects would gradually fade as rural people would hopefully find a decent way out of their dire predicament of penury of the company

7. WOW- Wealth out of waste

ITC has decided to step up its waste paper collection business under its WOW (Wealth out of Waste) program, to augment raw material supply for its paper board mills. ITC uses about 1.8 lakh ton of imported waste paper annually at its mills in Coimbatore and Bhadrachalam. According to company officials, it needs about 3 lakh tons of waste paper annually. The balance is sourced domestically. The company views the WOW program as an opportunity to step up domestic raw material availability.

As part of the program, now on in the four southern States, it has tied up with Ramky Infrastructure to launch door-to-door domestic waste collection. The company takes the paper-based materials for its own use and the other waste is recycled through tie-ups with other recyclers. According to Mr. B. Joga Rao, Vice-President (Commercial), ITC (Paperboards and Specialty Papers Division), the company now collects about 3,000 ton of waste paper a month, through the WOW program. It plans to increase collection to about 5,000 tons a month in April, and by the year end, to about 10,000 tons.

WOW is now on in five cities including Hyderabad and Visakhapatnam in Andhra Pradesh; Chennai, Coimbatore and Madurai in Tamil Nadu; Bangalore and Kochi.

The company plans to extend the program to other cities and is targeting educational institutions as well, In Hyderabad, it has implemented the program in seven schools and plans to launch it in 25 more. Children will be taught the value of recycling– one ton of paper produced from recycled material saves 22 trees, he said.

As countries across the globe increase recycling of waste paper for conservation needs and cost benefits, Indian paper manufacturers, who depend on imported waste paper, are increasingly feeling the pinch of waste paper shortage and increasing costs. According to ITC officials, the price of waste paper had increased by 30-40 per cent in the last three months to around Rs9,000-9,500 a ton.ITC has also tied up with around 100 companies to procure their waste paper.

Imported waste paper prices have been spiraling, as developed countries and major producers such as China are cutting back on virgin wood for paper production and increasing the use of waste paper as a raw material. China, which imports around 26 million ton of waste paper annually, is expected to use 6 million tons more as it steps up recycling. The US and Europe are also encouraging paper manufacturers to increase recycled content in paper.

India uses about 9 million tons of paper annually but only about 10 per cent of that is recycled, because of the absence of organized collection systems and low awareness of segregating waste at source. When paper waste mixes with other organic waste it cannot be used for recycling and is truly "wasted," industry experts said. India now imports close to 5 million tons of waste paper to produce a range of products.

ITC Sonar first hotel to earn carbon credits

ITC Hotels has set a precedence by possibly becoming the first hospitality chain in the world to have earned carbon credits. Its luxury property, ITC Sonar in Kolkata, which switched to energy efficient CFL bulbs as part of its energy saving drive, has been issued 1,996 carbon credits per annum for a period of 10 years. The project has been registered as a clean development mechanism project (CDM) at the United Nations Framework Convention on Climate Change(UNFCCC).

The carbon credits earned by the hotel through its energy efficiency process can be capitalized to add to its revenues. One carbon credit is equivalent to reduction of one ton of carbon-di-oxide. Carbon credits are currently trading at around euro 12 per unit. However, ITC has no immediate plans to sell its carbon credits as the price is currently low. The hotel had applied to the CDM executive board with total reductions of 2,987 metric ton of carbon dioxide per annum. However, the hotel qualified to earn 1,996 carbon credits per annum.

India's second largest hospitality chain brought on board international consultancy firm Price water house-Coopers to measure its carbon footprint and ITC Sonar, which was unveiled in 2002, was selected as a pilot project. The 238-room hotel has been using energy-conserving CFL bulbs and energy-efficient air conditioning appliances, solar water heating equipment and improved pumping systems, among other such initiatives.

"The journey to reduce greenhouse gas emissions is going on. The same will be reflected at all ITC properties," said Tarun Chattopadhyay, chief engineer of ITC Sonar. "ITC Sonar is the first hotel in the world to have earned carbon credits," he said. PwC is also in the process of mapping carbon footprint at ITC's other properties. ITC Hotels operates the ITC Luxury Collection, ITC Sheraton, Fortune and Welcome Heritage brands under its umbrella.

Globally, even though other hotels such as Four Seasons, Mandarin Oriental, Ritz-Carlton, Taj and Leela have been implementing eco-friendly measures, ITC is probably the first to earn carbon credits. Some like Starwood have even launched green hotels called 'Element'. The CDM fund expected from the project activity is expected to encourage Indian hotels for investing in energy efficient initiative which would contribute towards meeting the energy demand of the country at large

Conclusions:

The ITC has focus on various Marketing strategies an according to which they have made in their marketing strategies, these are:

A) Sourcing Capability– ITC has strong sourcing capabilities. With the help of various sources, ITC was able to extend its business in different sectors.

   They entered into FMCG after establishing a strong base in the agricultural sector.

   The wheat from the agricultural sector held in establishing a market for the Ashirvaadaata. Similarly, ITC used its various sources very effectively and efficiently.

B) Effective Brand Utilisation-After getting recognized in the agricultural & FMCG sector, ITC used its established brand name for entering into the stationary market.

They introduced classmate by ITC which helped them in grabbing a good market share.

Know how to do effective Business Branding.

C) Related Businesses-ITC had very interrelated businesses. This helped them in the in-house production of their raw materials.

For example, ITC used its paperboard business for the packaging of its various products. It reduced the costs & need for outsourcing.

D) Role of Management-Management is the heart and soul of a successful business. Having a leader like YC Deveshwar helped ITC in reaching heights.

E) Focus on Sustainability– ITC focuses on sustainability as its goal. Major projects of ITC are focusing on Sustainability.

They have targeted majorly those sectors which are sustainable in the long run, offering more growth.

F) Meeting Corporate Social Responsibility (CSR)– ITC focuses on fulfilling its social responsibility. This aspect is very important in today's scenario.

They started serving the society in Sarapaka, an economically backward area in Andhra Pradesh.ITC contributed to the development in education, environmental protection & community development.

Case Questions:

Q.1 How do you assess the Business Strategy and Corporate

Social Responsibility Policy of ITC -Are they completely in Sync or ITC has sacrificed many business growth opportunities due to its tag of Manufacturing so called sin products like Cigarettes.

Q.2 Why is ITC (Indian Tobacco Company) not changing its Brand name from ITC to any other name which will detach its association with Tobacco products.?

Q.3 Are there any hidden factors such as near monopoly in Tobacco products and sentiments and lac of Competitive Advantage which prevent ITC from Entering High Technology products such as Auto Industry and Internet Technology products?

Q.4 What are your comments on ITC being able to retain its respectfully managed company in spite of losing on product brand image.?

22. Great Thought --Difficult For Business

A Case Study in Sustainability Management

Learning objectives

It has been always a catch 22 situation for majority of projects in Sustainability Management irrespective of considerations on economic , environmental, Societal sustainability issues ,There has always been string resistence all such projects within and between the essential aspects of Sustainability Management. It has mostly been a difficult tradeoff between Growth or Sustainability priorities in conflict with each other

Synopsis:

People watch the actions of leaders, and it resonates, says Mr. Albanese, the soft spoken former top gun at the $47.7 billion mining giant Rio Tinto, who completes one year as CEO of Vedanta group an Indian conglomerate in mining sector. In the implementation and measurement of corporate sustainability the **'Tone from the Top'** is critical, especially while attempting to usher in a fundamental change in the corporate culture of a company, which is perhaps the most reviled in global attempts to managing for sustainability.

Over the years, Vedanta has been mauled by civil society campaigns over its human rights record, in India and elsewhere, and has also incurred the wrath of large global investors. According to Albanese, who has issued notes to key levels of management that his two 'no-compromise positions are safety and integrity' even as he looks deeper in to the tenets of responsible mining and sustainable development at Vedanta Group.

Senior management at Vedanta also recognizes that Vedanta's social license to operate has been frayed and that it is about time to retrieve the situation. "We have been unable to operate at our full capacities," says Albanese, underlining the need to regain trust and the societal license. There is indeed a strong business case to be responsible Corporate Social Responsibility (CSR) measures are certainly welcome, but it can only be a small component of an overall approach. While Albanese is deeply appreciative of Vedanta's CSR programs, he is clearly uncomfortable with the charity of approach; the idea of creating a 'dependency relationship' between a company and communities.

Arvind Khare of the US-based Rights and Resources Initiative speaks in the same vein and explains that the Indian Land Acquisition Bill will do little to ameliorate conflicts in India as long as the legitimate claims of communities on forests, wastelands, commons or pastures are not recognized

Today Vedants needs a very refined approach to sustainable mining. The company should mandate 'cultural heritage assessments,' of mining sites. It even should seek 'disturbance approval' from communities, with an non compromising objective that indigenous peoples ought to be the 'drivers of their own destinies' and that they have 'a share in the wealth generated by mining activities.'

The Vedanta story would have been quite different if it had a degree of sensitivity to the cultural traditions of the Dongria-Kondhs who venerate the Niyamgiri hills in India as their god.

What Vedanta Claims:

Our Approach

Our vision is to be a leading, diversified natural resources company providing superior returns to our shareholders – a journey we have been on for a decade. We will meet our vision by delivering high-quality assets and low-cost operations, with sustainable development at the core of all that we do.

Our Strategy

We aim to deliver growth and long-term value while upholding sustainable development through our diversified portfolio of large, long-life and low-cost assets. Our Sustainability Model, which comprises the three pillars of Responsible Stewardship, Building Strong Relationships and Adding and Sharing Value, provides us with a robust structure for driving our future growth, advancing our business outcomes and offering significant benefits to the communities that host our operations.

Our Sustainability Model

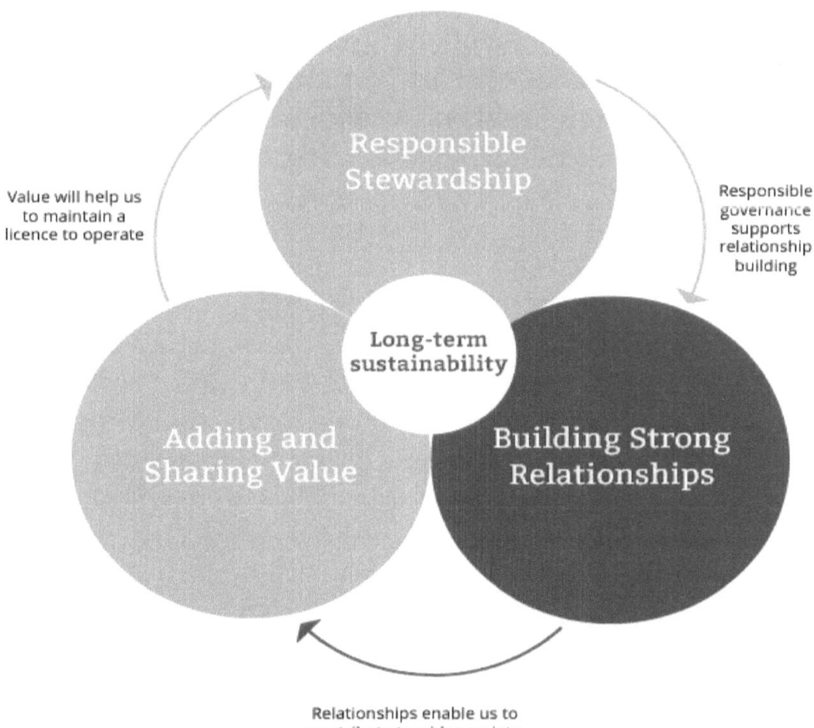

Responsible Stewardship means ensuring we have effective and appropriate business processes, including robust compliance and risk management, protecting the health and safety of our employees and responsibly managing our environmental and social impacts.

Building Strong Relationships captures our engagement with the people and organisations that are interested in our business. Doing this effectively can lead to the identification of new areas where we can find and unlock additional value as well as equipping us to foresee and appropriately manage challenges.

Adding and Sharing Value encapsulates the direct and indirect positive economic impact we make, by investing in people through employment, building infrastructure, developing technology and the payment of taxes, royalties and other payments to local, state and national governments. Additionally, it captures the value we offer by turning the knowledge and ideas sourced through engagement with our stakeholders into specific projects, including collaborating with governments and NGOs to bring value to the communities that host our operations.

Our three pillars guide our stakeholder engagement and help us to build trusted relationships. As a consequence of these engagements and to respond to stakeholders' areas of interest we developed our Sustainability Framework. The Framework comprises policies, technical standards, management standards and guidance notes across the three pillars to establish clear standards, set targets for improving performance and maximise value to our stakeholders.

Since introducing our sustainability model and supporting Sustainability Framework in 2011-12, we have implemented our policies, standards and processes across the Group.

Community at the Centre

Albanese the new CEO of Vedanta says it was unfortunate that Vedanta allowed the Niyamgiri issue to fester and turn 'iconic.' Communities, with greater mobile and net access, are more aware of and are standing up for their rights. International institutions are pitching in with binding and voluntary norms: the ILO Convention 169, the UN Declaration on the Rights of Indigenous Peoples, the UN Principles on Human Rights and Businesses and more recently, the revised IFC performance standards.

Albanese is therefore endeavoring to align the company to emerging global trends in responsibility — be it human rights, bio-diversity protection or the growing traction on Free Prior and Informed Consent — while dealing with land and communities.He is also taking Vedanta into the International Council on Mining and Metals (ICMM), which is focused on the sustainability performance of extractive companies. The ICMM as a standards setting out fit has catalyzed improvements in the extractive sector. Last year, for instance, around 15% of its membership vowed to consider the 'no-go' option, even for prospecting, in areas of high biodiversity value. Can Vedanta, considering where it is today, absorb and measure up to global sustainability standards? Albanese is certain it can, for it has performed reasonably well in certain aspects of sustainability. "If a company is weak in any individual part of sustainability, everything falls apart," he says. He is also aware that it will take time for the transformation to happen; that is the reason why he is pacing the process and working on multiple fronts. On taking over as CEO he didn't try a bring- down-and-rebuild approach."Bending and moulding is my way," he says.

Also demonstrating sustainability leadership immediately on taking over he made it clear that safety and integrity would be the corner stone of his drive. Employees are perplexed when he frowns on people who don't use the support rails while climbing or coming down flights of stairs.

A Fresh Perspective

Safety is a huge challenge for the group. The chimney collapse, which saw the death of 45 people at the Balco plant in Korba in 2009 still rankles. Vedanta recorded 19 fatal accidents in 2013-14. It's down to five this year; eight including the Konkola Copper Mines in Zambia (while Rio Tinto with operations in 40 countries had only three fatalities in the same period). Albanese wants to move to a zero-fatalities scenario.

While internally there is a new engagement with employees, both chairman Agarwal and Albanese are sending signals about the shift in attitudes to outside stakeholders too. The duo has made it clear that the company will not mine in areas 'without the express invitation and free prior agreement of the local communities to do so. While a court process has already seen the Niyamgiri palli sabhas say 'no' to bauxite mining, the unambiguous proclamation and stand on 'consent' is an attempt to 'create a cleaner picture around brand Vedanta.'

It's still work in progress. The stranglehold of people from accounting, finance and engineering on company matters is, or was, complete and absolute in Vedanta. This had to be broken to engender some sensitivity towards sustainable development. One may acquire the cognitive skills but may not get the lateral bandwidth; the full intuitive understanding of a resources company. Expanding this bandwidth to embrace views not just from these narrow confines can lead to change. Explains Albanese-We now look at issues from a fresh set of eyes and what precisely are the sustainability issues most relevant to the company? To get a hold on this, a materiality mapping was done. As expected safety, waste, water, emissions, community management, approach to new projects were high priority.

The surprise element in the matrix was the need to address biodiversity issues. For most Indian companies, bio diversity does not figure on the agenda but it's gaining traction globally.

For mining companies, biodiversity conservation is integral to securing the social license to operate. (Rio Tinto pursues a policy of Net Positive Impact -NPI, which refers to a point where biodiversity gains exceed biodiversity loss due to mining or other project activities).

Albanese concedes that NPI is extremely difficult and can only be asp rational for many as he recalls the complex modeling and biodiversity offset principles he had to wade through in his previous job. For Vedanta, he prescribes a policy of 'No Net Loss' in the mitigation hierarchy (NNL ensures there is no overall reduction in the type, amount and condition of biodiversity over space and time).

Albanese is also passionate about transparency and would like to soon emulate an industry first from his previous company; reporting on the economic contributions made by a company to public finances; all listed out in the most granular fashion. A quick scan of the company's 20-page tax paid report of 2014 reveals that Rio Tinto, with a very marginal presence in India (the Bunder project), paid $4 million in taxes to the Indian government and $1 million to Madhya Pradesh ,a 'tax paid report' is a valuable document; it allows you to engage with stakeholders on this vital issue," says Albanese.

For Vedanta, which has faced tax demands in Zambia, and continues to face them in India, some sunshine on taxes paid is welcome. The sustainability agenda is clearly kicking in it looks like?

With Global Sustainability regulations getting very stringent how would Vedanta be able to take a leadership role in its Sustainability management efforts is yet to be seen, The Political will and the regulatory controls as resisted by the clouded understanding of simultaneous management of sustainability and Growth are the real challenges for Min ing Industries   in India.While issues such as a forestation and dislocation of Aadi vasis from their naturalized habitats are being partly real and partly created and fully exploited by the middlemen it looks a real uphill task for India to raise to the call of Global Community towards ensuring sustainability on the Planet Earth.

Even the CSR norms as revised in the recent amendments to the Companies act and the Listing agreements are being contested for clarity and attempts to find loop holes in the law are rampant as ever. There is already a great hue and cry about the amendments to the land acquisition bill in the governmental levels and its easy for the land mafias to exploit the situation to the detriment of the common man and his sustainable future. Projects with high promise of economic growth literally each one of them need to be vetted by sustainability clause unless there is clarity of understanding of objectives and impacts of sustainability measures from a very very long term points of view devoid of greed and small mind approach to prosperity through improved quality of life Individual entities like Vedanta will continue to face the proverbial Catch 22 Situation blamed for noncompliance and equally guilty of following the socio political hidden agenda.

Some Food for Thoughts on sustainable Management

Costs of conflict

The study, conducted by the Harvard Kennedy School and the Centre for Social Responsibility in Mining, Australia, indicate a world class mining project (capital expenditure between $3 billion and $5 billion) stands to lose approximately $20 million per week of delayed production in Net Present Value (NPV) due to lost sales arising out of conflicts.

It was also revealed that fire-fighting after things have gone terribly wrong in the project life cycle is not the right approach as the relationship with the community, even if mended, can be fragile. Engagement and measures to prevent conflict have to happen before the start of the project.

Another recent study by the Washington DC-based Rights and Resources Initiative reveals land issues that lead to social conflict can increase operating costs of companies by as much as 29 times over a baseline scenario. The situation is indeed grim as future global reserves are largely spread over indigenous peoples' or tribal lands; 50% for oil and gas production and 80% for mining. In India, a quarter of the districts are already affected . Conflicts will only increase, says Arvind Khare, executive director, Rights and Resources Group of the Initiative.

Free prior and informed consent

While the present government attempts to water down consent requirements in the Land Acquisition Bill and other laws, the world, including large mining and oil and gas corporations, is headed in the opposite direction.

The concept of Free Prior and Informed Consent (FPIC), while dealing with tribal or indigenous communities is gaining traction in national law, international norms, and voluntary best practice standards. Land rights therefore have moved beyond the realms of narrow social justice debates. It's now all about democratic rights, equity-driven economic development and environmental sustainability. FPIC, as the term suggests, is much more nuanced than consultation or plain-vanilla consent. Iterations are still being debated but it is generally agreed that FPIC also lends indigenous communities the right to say 'no' to a project or even refrain from engaging on the issue. The financial sector is also cleaning up its act. The IFC of the World Bank Group, in its revised performance standards, embraces FPIC.

This automatically brings in over 80 financial institutions in 35 countries that have signed up for the 'Equator Principles' into the fold. The Equator banks cover 70% of international project fi nance debt in emerging markets. The FPIC guidelines of the International Council for Mining & Metals, with almost all major global mining corporations as members, comes into effect from May 2015. The sticky part, however, emerges when national standards are lower than FPIC as is the situation in India. How do multinationals navigate this issue? Tom Albanese, Vedanta CEO, is guarded, and maintains mining companies cannot override national legislation or impinge on the sovereign rights of a country.

The international community has addressed this issue. For instance, the UN special rapporteur on indigenous peoples' rights has clarified that companies must respect the rights of indigenous peoples even 'in cases where states are opposed to the application of making FPIC a reality.'

Coexistence and benefit sharing

For over 40 years, the aboriginal communities of Weipa in Australia were in constant skirmish with the mining company Comalco (now Rio Tinto Alcan). The region constitutes one of the world's largest bauxite reserves covering 3860 sq km. A truce emerged only in 2001 with the signing of the Western Cape Communities Co-existence Agreement (WCCCA) between the company, the communities of the region, local councils and the Queensland government. It took them five years of hard negotiations. At the signing ceremony, the acting CEO of the company Keith Johnson promised a fresh beginning and apologized to the communities for taking four decades to realize they could co-exist and prosper together.

The WCCCA goes beyond recognizing land, jobs and rehabilitation rights; it also includes cultural heritage and environment protection, land relinquishment plans and outlines governance structures. Most importantly, it also spells out an extensive benefit sharing program with the company contributing a minimum of $2.5 million a year and more depending on bauxite production and the market price of Aluminium.

Another $ 500,000 a year is spent on capacity building of communities; education, skills training and now even entrepreneurship development and supplier diversity initiatives. The Queensland government contributes another $1.5 million a year. Around $6 million is invested into the Weipa communities each year. The monies come into a Communities Trust and 60% of the funds are immediately locked up in long- term secure investments so that future generations also benefit. The mines are expected to be productive for another 40 years. The remaining 40% of the funds is distributed to three sub-regional trusts, which oversee community projects of different aboriginal groups. The entire system is designed to involve direct participation of the communities in the decision-making processes. This is not all. The bouquet of Weipa agreements includes the Weipa Township Agreement: Rio Tinto Alcan is responsible for administering the Weipa town. Obviously, there have been challenges in Weipa but through the years course corrections have happened as businesses and governments now realize that social investments are more than risk mitigation measures..

Case Questions:

Q1. How should one look in to Sustainability issues in Emerging Markets? There is appears to be a greater dimension than globalization to the localized issues of poverty, security and safety in the garb of corruption, exploitation and fundamentalistic approaches overriding the calls of the Planet for Pollution control and sustainable Business Practices

Q2 Most of us are aware of the violent demonstrations which took place recently at Vedanta's Sterlite Project in Tamil Nadu after running successfully for 20 years Sterlite unit has been shut closed .Similarly the Major Oil refinery project in Maharashtra(Konkan Area) is being opposed tooth and nail by locals as also by prominent political parties. Same applies to Samruddha Express way and the Bullet Train Project. How can growth be achieved without Infra Projects?

Q3 How should India handle the dilemma of Growth Vs Sustainability Development?

23. Liar, Liar: Is 'Apple' on Fire?

A Case Study on sustaining Competitive Advantage

Learning objectives:

a) To provide world with the best innovations and technologies in the world.

b) To find out the success recipe for new product development and how companies make good advantage of the success recipe.

c) Understanding the relation between culture and innovations.

d) To ensure good health and safety of the company's employees, customers and the global communities.

Synopsis:

The New World Encyclopedia (2018) states that Apple Inc., formerly Apple Computer, Inc., is a multinational corporation that creates consumer electronics, personal computers, servers, and computer software, and is a digital distributor of media content. The company also has a chain of retail stores known as Apple Stores. Apple's core product lines are the iPhone, iPod, and Macintosh computer. Founders Steve Jobs and Steve Wozniak created Apple Computer on April 1, 1976, and incorporated the company on January 3, 1977, in Cupertino, California.

For more than three decades, Apple Computer was predominantly a manufacturer of personal computers, including the Apple II, Macintosh, and Power Mac lines, but it faced rocky sales and low market share during the 1990s.

Jobs, who had been ousted from the company in 1985, returned to Apple in 1996 after his company next was bought by Apple. The following year he became the company's interim CEO, which later became permanent. Jobs subsequently instilled a new corporate philosophy of recognizable products and simple design, starting with the original iMac in 1998.

With the introduction of the successful iPod music player in 2001 and iTunes Music Store in 2003, Apple established itself as a leader in the consumer electronics and media sales industries, leading it to drop "Computer" from the company's name in 2007. The Company sells and delivers digital content and applications through the iTunes Store, App Store, Mac App Store, television APP Store, iBook's Store and Apple Music (collectively Internet Services).

The Company sells its products through its retail stores, online stores and direct sales force through third-party cellular network carriers, wholesalers, retailers and value-added resellers. The Company sells a range of third-party Apple compatible products, including application software and accessories through its retail and online stores. The Company sells to consumers, small and mid-sized businesses and education, enterprise and government customers.

Cloud is the Company's cloud service, which stores music, photos, contacts, calendars, mail, documents and more, keeping them up-to-date and available across multiple iOS devices, Mac and Windows personal computers and Apple TV. iCloud services includes Drive, Photo Library, Family Sharing, Find My iPhone, iPad or Mac, Find My Friends, Notes, iCloud Keychain and I Cloud Backup for iOS devices. AppleCare offers a range of support options for the Company's customers. The cult of Apple is strong. Or was it? Consumers are not happy. And when consumers are not happy, the survival of a company is in jeopardy… and Apple is now being accused of programmed obsolescence.

Case Contents

Bra shares (2001) tell us that Apple Computers, Inc. was founded on April 1, 1976, by college dropouts Steve Jobs and Steve Wozniak, who brought to the new company a vision of changing the way people, viewed computers. Jobs and Wozniak wanted to make computers small enough for people to have them in their homes or offices. Simply put, they wanted a computer that was user-friendly.

The two Steve's - Jobs and Wozniak - may have been Apple's most visible founders, but were it not for their friend Ronald Wayne there might be no iPhone, iPad or iMac today. Jobs convinced him to take 10% of the company stock and act as an arbiter should he and Wozniak come to blows, but Wayne backed out 12 days later, selling for just $500 a holding that would have been worth $72bn 40 years later. (Rawlinson, 2017).Woz produced the first computer with a typewriter-like keyboard and the ability to connect to a regular TV as a screen. Later christened the Apple I, it was the archetype of every modern computer, but Wozniak wasn't trying to change the world with what he'd produced - he just wanted to show off how much he'd managed to do with so few resources.

Speaking to Byte magazine in December 1984, Woz credited Jobs with the idea. "He was working from time to time in the orchards up in Oregon. I thought that it might be because there were apples in the orchard or maybe just its fruitarian nature. Maybe the word just happened to occur to him. In any case, we both tried to come up with better names but neither one of us could think of anything better after Apple was mentioned."

According to the biography of Steve Jobs, the name was conceived by Jobs after he returned from apple farm. He apparently thought the name sounded "fun, spirited and not intimidating". The name also likely benefitted by beginning with an A, which meant it would be nearer the front of any listings.

Apple and Microsoft

If it was a soap opera, Apple and Microsoft's on-off relationship would put many to shame. Today, you'd never guess there had ever been anything wrong, and that's probably down to the fact that their relationship has never been more symbiotic.

Weinberger (2017) tells Fast forward to 1996, when Jobs appeared in a PBS documentary called "Triumph of the Nerds" and just ripped into Gates and Microsoft, saying that they make "third-rate products". Jobs went on in that same documentary: "The only problem with Microsoft is they just have no taste. They have absolutely no taste. And I don't mean that in a small way, I mean that in a big way, in the sense that they don't think of original ideas, and they don't bring much culture into their products."

By 1997, Jobs was Apple CEO. At his first Macworld keynote, he announced that he had accepted an investment from Microsoft to keep Apple afloat. Bill Gates appeared on a huge screen via satellite uplink. The audience booed. Gates clearly admired Jobs, even if they didn't always see eye to eye. When Apple introduced iTunes, Gates sent an internal email to Microsoft that said "Steve Jobs' ability to focus in on a few things that count, get people who get user interface right, and market things as revolutionary are amazing things."

Wikipedia describes the movie "Pirates of Silicon Valley "as an original 1999 American made for television biographical drama film, directed by Martin Burke and starring Noah Wyle as Steve Jobs and Anthony Michael Hall as Bill Gates. Spanning the years 1971–1997 and based on Paul Freiberg and Michael Swine's 1984 book Fire in the Valley: The Making of the Personal Computer, it explores the impact of the rivalry between Jobs

(Apple Computer) and Gates (Microsoft) on the development of the personal computer.

Rozsa (2015) said that: "unfortunately, there was a darker side to the PC revolution, which is why the word "Pirates" appears in the title of "Pirates of Silicon Valley." While Jobs and Gates were indisputably brilliant men, they did not invent much of the technology that is widely attributed to them.

No, the credit for those innovations belongs to countless obscure men and women – many of them employees at Xerox, which paid them to create marvels and then refused to make bank on their work because it didn't appreciate what they had. Jobs realized this and, characteristically, charmed Xerox into forcing its resentful employees to share the fruits of their labor's with the self-entitled Jobs, who thought nothing of harvesting their bounty and acting like he had cultivated it himself.

This brings us to the other scene that captures the essence of this movie's greatness, an exchange between Jobs and Gates after the former realizes the latter has been stealing his innovations (much as Jobs did to the hapless Xerox employees), which I dare not quote here for risk of spoiling it for others. Suffice to say this much: This is as much a film about intellectual theft, and the grandiose egotism necessary to morally justify such actions, as it is about genius and inspiration and the world-changing technology they wrought."

Burying hatchets:

IDC figures released in summer 2015 showed Mac sales to have climbed by 16% over the previous quarter. At the same time, though, the overall PC market for machines running Windows had dipped by 11.8%. So, with ever more of Microsoft's revenue coming from Office 365, it needs to push its subscription-based productivity service onto as many platforms as it can - including Android, iOS and, of course, the Mac.

Apple, on the other hand, needs Office. It has its own productivity apps in the shape of Pages, Numbers and Keynote, but Word, Excel and PowerPoint remain more or less industry standards, so if it's going to be taken seriously in the business world, Apple needs Microsoft Office on board.

So, a peace has broken out - and a long-lasting one at that, which despite some sniping from either side, stretches right back to Jobs' return to Apple after his time at NeXT.(We'll come to that later), but suffice it to say at this point that it shouldn't really surprise us: the rivalry between the two camps often seems overblown. Microsoft developed many of the Office apps for the Mac before porting them to the PC and, in the early days at least,

Bill Gates had good things to say about the company. "To create a new standard, it takes something that's not just a little bit different," he said in 1984, "it takes something that's really new, and really captures people's imagination. And the Macintosh - of all the machines I've seen - is the only one that meets that standard."

That's pretty flattering, but there's a saying about flattery: imitation is its sincerest form. Apple apparently didn't see it that way when Microsoft, in Apple's eyes, went on to imitate its products a little too faithfully. As we already know, Apple had been inspired by certain elements of an operating system it saw at Xerox PARC when it was developing the Macintosh and Lisa. Xerox's implementation used the desktop metaphor now familiar to OS X, Windows and many Linux users, and when Microsoft was developing Windows 1.0, Apple licensed some of its fundamentals to the company that Jobs latterly took to calling "our friends up north".

In 2014, Microsoft named its top cloud computing executive, Satya Nadella, as chief executive on .The Company also said Bill Gates would step aside as chairman of the board but would remain a technology adviser to the company. John Thompson, who has been the lead independent director, becamechairman.

Nadella's appointment ends a longer-than-expected search for a new leader after Steve Ballmer the Microsoft former CEO, announced his intention to retire in August of 2013.Nadella is only the third CEO in Microsoft's 39-year history, following co-founder Bill Gates and Ballmer. Before Microsoft, the Indian-born executive worked at Sun Microsystems.

The famously ebullient Ballmer -- who joined Microsoft in 1980 as the company's first business manager and rose quickly through the ranks -- leaves the company after 13 difficult years as CEO. The company was once the most valuable in the world, but Microsoft has lost more than half of its market value over the past decade.

With Nadella, the tables have turned in the Microsoft-Apple rivalry. For decades, Apple had but a sliver of the market share for personal computers. In 2014, Apple was not only shipping more personal computers – counting the ones that fit in our pockets – It was making much more money from them. Apple made $156 billion in revenue from iPhones, iPads and Macs in the last year. And Microsoft? Between Windows and Office software, Nokia phones and Surface tablets, it saw about $23 billion in revenue.

Steve Jobs Era:

Apple's popularity exploded in the 2000s. The iPod, smaller and sleeker with each generation, introduced many lifelong Windows users to their first Apple gadget. The arrival of the iTunes music store in 2003 gave people a convenient way to buy music legally online, song by song. For the music industry, it was a mixed blessing. The industry got a way to reach Internet-savvy people who, in the age of Napster, were growing accustomed to downloading music free. But online sales also hastened the demise of CDs and established Apple as a gatekeeper, resulting in battles between Jobs and music executives over pricing and other issues.

Jobs' command over gadget lovers and pop culture swelled to the point that, on the eve of the iPhone's launch in 2007, faithful followers slept on sidewalks outside posh Apple stores for the chance to buy one.

Three years later, at the iPad's debut, the lines snaked around blocks and out through parking lots, even though people had the option to order one in advance.

Perhaps most influentially, Jobs in 2001 launched the iPod, which offered "1,000 songs in your pocket." Over the next 10 years, its white earphones and thumb-dial control seemed to become more ubiquitous than the wristwatch.

In 2007 came the touch-screen iPhone, joined a year later by Apple's App Store, where developers could sell iPhone "apps" which made the phone a device not just for making calls but also for managing money, editing photos, playing games and social networking. And in 2010, Jobs introduced the iPad, a tablet-sized, all-touch computer that took off even though market analysts said no one really needed one.

By 2011, Apple had become the second-largest company of any kind in the United States by market value. In August, it briefly surpassed Exxon Mobil as the most valuable company. Under Jobs, the company cloaked itself in secrecy to build frenzied anticipation for each of its new products. Jobs himself had a wizardly sense of what his customers wanted, and where demand didn't exist, he leveraged a cult-like following to create it.

When he spoke at Apple presentations, almost always in faded blue jeans, sneakers and a black mock turtleneck, legions of

Apple acolytes listened to every word. He often boasted about Apple successes, then coyly added a code— "one more thing" — before introducing its latest ambitious idea.

In later years, Apple investors also watched these appearances for clues about his health. Jobs revealed in 2004 that he had been diagnosed with a very rare form of pancreatic cancer — an islet cell neuroendocrine tumour. He underwent surgery and said he had been cured.

In 2009, following weight loss he initially attributed to a hormonal imbalance, he abruptly took a six-month leave. During that time, he received a liver transplant that became public two months after it was performed.

He went on another medical leave in January 2011, this time for an unspecified duration. He never went back and resigned as CEO in August, though he stayed on as chairman. Consistent with his penchant for secrecy, he didn't reference his illness in his resignation letter.

Post-Steve Jobs Era:

Apple's creative director Hugh Dubberly was concerned that Apple is in danger of being left behind by Samsung now that the company is in the post Steve Jobs era. Apple's biggest strategic mistake since Steve Jobs' death has been to concede the power-user market. Apple no longer makes anything that could be regarded as a high-end workstation. Apple has only the (trashcan) Mac Pro, which has been a bit of a disaster. That machine is too constrained to have general purpose utility.

The most powerful iMacs cannot support a desktop class GPU.

Nevertheless, Tim Cook is succeeding at an impossible task: Following the greatest-ever product visionary as Apple's CEO. Yet six years after his mentor Steve Jobs died, Apple is thriving.

And Cook is growing into his prominence as one of the business world's most increasingly vocal good-guy CEOs.

For Apple, 2017 was a return to growth. After sales declines in 2016, Apple has now posted four consecutive quarters of year-over-year revenue gains — and it's accelerating. The Apple Watch, the first major new product launched under the Cook era, has quietly become a big hit. Air Pods are amazing and exciting. Together, they form a wearable computer line up that has many interesting applications, notably fitness and medicine. Cook and company are also setting Apple up to succeed in augmented reality — where real life and computer graphics are mixed— which many see as one of the next big technology waves.

Apple has a group of loyal users in the academic community. It has loyal users in the visual effects community and loyal users in game development & VR. There are even a significant number of common-or-garden software developers, all of whom would gladly pay-out for a machine with lots of RAM, lots of cores, and a giant smoking GPU. But there is a problem: by not offering a suitable machine for these users, Apple has burned a pile of good will with its most influential (and wealthiest) customers.

In pure commercial terms, there is absolutely nothing wrong with this decision. The amount of actual revenue this market represents is less than a rounding error on Apple's bottom line. By dropping the top-end machines, Apple's engineers can focus on other products which really do generate profits. The return on investment for high end workstations will be far less than phones, consumer computers or even watch bands.

The Criticism on Apple

In the last few years, Apple has been struggling with complaints from all over the world. India, France, Italy, South Korea, China… and this is just exploding. Apple is accused of much dubious behaviour. For instance, they have been claimed by critics to combine stolen and/or purchased designs that it claims are its own original creations; unethical business practices such as anti-competitive behaviour , rash litigation, and dubious tax tactics, their production methods involving the use of sweatshop labour, customer service issues involving misleading warranties and insufficient data security, and concerns about environmental destruction.

Additionally, it has been criticized for its alleged collaboration with U.S. surveillance program, PRISM. Later, they denied knowing about this issue. In YouTube, there are some short documentaries talking about how many workers from manufacturers for Apple, are getting cancer. It is related with benzene poisoning and how they develop occupational cancer.

But in spite of these awful situations, the slowdown of older iPhones is the most scandalous yet expensive complaint for Apple. Apple has accepted some responsibility of it and right now (2018) the company is trying to solve this situation. Apple acknowledged on December of 2017, that the iPhone software had the effect of slowing down some phones with battery problems, but denied that it had ever done anything to intentionally shorten the life of a product.

The firm apologized for its actions and cut battery replacement costs. It has also said it would change its software to show users whether their phone batteries were working well. On December 28th, Apple apologized, but nearly 67,000 iPhone users in Korea have applied to join a lawsuit against Apple as the company admitted to deliberately slowing down the performance of older models to prolong battery life.

At least 15 class action cases have been filed against Apple in the US and international markets. The one in France, which holds the potential of criminal charges, seems to be the most dangerous one, while the one in the US that asks for nearly a trillion dollars in damage is the funniest one. Lawsuits have been filed against Apple in California, New York and Illinois alleging the company defrauded users by slowing down devices without warning.

The company also faces a legal complaint in France, where so-called "planned obsolescence" is against the law. Lomas (2018) mentions that Programmed obsolescence is illegal in France under a 2015 law which prohibits "the use of techniques by which the person responsible for the marketing of a product aims to deliberately reduce the duration to increase the replacement rate ".The law carries a penalty of a maximum sentence of two years in prison and up to 5 per cent of a company's annual turnover.

However the firm said: "We have never - and would never - does anything to intentionally shorten the life of any Apple product, or degrade the user experience to drive customer upgrades."

Apple's strategy to re-establish customer's satisfaction

In South Korea, Apple has said that as part of its next update, expected in March of 2018, it will give users the option to turn off the feature that slows down the older handsets. The firm has already reduced the price of any out-of-warranty iPhone 6 or later battery replacements, by more than half.

Ian Morris (2017) a Forbes Media contributor explains: Firstly, Apple will replace the batteries in older phones for a greatly reduced price. The company will drop this service from $79 to $29. This will apply to anyone who has an iPhone 6 or later and will be available for the next year - ending in December 2018.

Secondly, the company says that it will provide more battery information from within iOS. This will give users a clear indication if it is the age of their battery that is causing them problems. For some users, it will simply be issues with apps.

But the phone will make it clearer if a battery replacement would help or not.

The third step is to look at how Apple manages the phones themselves. If the customer had an unexpected shutdown then he/she might find that a less than ideal way for your phone to work. So perhaps in future, we'll see the iPhone sending notifications to warn that the battery in the device needs replacing. Or perhaps offering a choice of slowing down the max performance to get a bit more power - a bit like the existing power saving mode.

The journalist Ramya Patel khan (2018), made a quite interesting interview to David Temin, an RP consultant, and spoke about how Apple can restore trust and the crisis management. Davia Temin said Apple's explanation for the battery slowdown is "perfectly adequate" but "too little, too late."

The explanation would've been acceptable before the issue arose or at the time of releasing updates that slowed devices. The explanation -forced by lawsuits, complaints, and information revealed by third-parties- is inadequate. Temin says despite the bad software update process, very few users lost trust in Apple. However, when iPhone owners understood that the upgrades were planned to slow their devices, without even informing them, their trust just "vanished."

The problem began some time ago, but Apple didn't truthfully address it. It issued an apology on December 28[th]through a spokesperson only after lawsuits were filed. Temin said for restoring trust Apple should first "revamp" the iPhone update process. She says users should be able to refuse updates; they shouldn't be forced or tricked into accepting updates. Before installation, users should be well-informed about what the update is for and the changes it brings.

Customers should have an option to undo or reverse an update if they don't like it.

Temin says Apple should get rid of "defensiveness, arrogance, or radio silence" and instead communicates clearly and truthfully with customers in the time of crisis. Whenever an issue arises, Apple must address it immediately before it gets exposed "by a third-party".

Whenever there's public outrage about something, Apple should try and repair the situation before it gets worse. It must detect and respond to such situations before the damage is done or before law forces it.

Temin said Apple should start holding an "on-going dialogue" with its users, adding the company should listen to people's concerns and then act on them. She also feels Apple must respond to every complaint it receives. She said Apple's associates, apart from those at support stations, must be empowered to send reports about the concerns or issues raised and also apologize when required. Also, the company must apologize "early, sincerely, and without prompt or caveat."

Davia Temin stated: "Readjust your (Apple) global attitude. Give people a reason to love and trust you again...if you don't, your franchise will erode. Only your competitors want that, not the fan base that desperately wants to be loyal...to see you continue to succeed."

Is it enough?

There are four reasons battery replacements could affect iPhoneX sales:

This incident has caused significantly higher public awareness of Apple's behavior, and thereby, the $29 offer.$29 is affordable, and it will provide a significant boost in speed (from 600MHz to 1400MHz for an iPhone 6).

Our August Wireless survey suggests battery drain is No.1

reason for users to upgrade to new device — therefore, a new battery may deter some upgrade intention.

Apple allows for replacement regardless of the diagnostic test result. Given the same form factor from IP6 to IP8, some customers may prefer the battery swap over upgrading.

Apple's fix for this problem was to limit the peak power draw that an older iPhone was capable of through software updates.

After it revealed the fix in December, people were furious to receive confirmation from Apple that older iPhones could take longer to launch apps, may display choppy scrolling, and could have dimmer screens and quieter speakers.

Apple now has to hope that iPhone users don't decide to take a $29 battery over a $999 iPhone X.

Conclusions:

1) Though Apple's strategic model cannot be said, to be distinct, they are poised on taking Amazon and Microsoft head on. Their new products for example, iPad, suggests to be a real one in all product for the consumers. Apple success factors suggest that they have the ability and capability to become the market leaders. The major success factor being innovation.

2) Behind their ability to innovate is its strong research and development department.

3) Its likely block chain innovations will assist identity and information protection strategies, as we›ll be far beyond using simple multifactor and even biometric protections.

4) The latest product of Apple, the iPad, however targeted on, the retired people and journalists, has received acceptance from the youth, students and the rest of the population giving Apple, a grab of the market.

Case questions:

Q1. How do you explain the Love hate relationship between Apple & Microsoft even though they had to mutually depend on each other even for snatched out technology from Xerox employees? Was this Business or personal rivalry between Steve and Gates?

Q2. What was the Korean companies the Samsung doing when Apple and Microsoft were busy building their empires in US. How could they suddenly shock the market almost dethroning these behemoths?

Q3. Do you suspect any role Samsung has in decrying Apple on Slow batteries complaint in the back ground of its own burnt fingers during Samsung S7 models catching fire & exploding which had almost black listed Samsung for a yearlong disaster at Market Place?

Q4. Why is Apple coming out clearly and boldly on to take up the issue of slowing down batteries in older models by clarifying the real reasons based onscientific investigations rather than offering battery replacement at 30% price reduction. Is Apple hiding more than its offer to come out clean??